NO OFFENSE, NO DEFENSE, NO HOPE!

How an Old-School Coach Transformed a College Football Team of Perennial Underdogs and Won a Championship for the Ages.

DAVID D. DODA

Cover Design by Brittany Becker, BrittLouise Creative

Interior Layout and Design by Brittany Becker, BrittLouise Creative

Paperback ISBN: 979-8-218-99018-3

Published by Amazon Kindle Direct Publishing (KDP) 4900 Lacross Road, North Charleston, SC 29406-6558

To my Demon Deacon teammates from the 1970 season. The bonds we forged through shared struggle, sacrifice and, ultimately, triumph, transcend conventional friendship. What we experienced as a team created a brotherhood that has withstood the test of time.

CONTENTS

Prologue. ix

1   Culture Shock 1

2   Gold, Black, and Brown 11

3   The Heart of Cal Stoll 17

4   Heads, Hearts, and Down-ups. 21

5   Old-School Football 27

6   The Intangibles 33

7   Glory Hallelujah 37

8   It Starts with a Winning Attitude 45

9   The Stoll Era Begins 49

10 The Drive-In Debacle 53

11 A Nation in Turmoil 57

12 A World of Possibility. 63

13 A Team with Heart 67

14 Breaking Barriers with a Pen 73

15 The Draft. 79

16 Starting Over: 1970 83

17 A Season of Civil Unrest. 89

18 The Puzzle. 97

19 New Year, New Mindset 103

20 Testing Our Mettle 107

21 Hope in the Face of Doubt 113

22 The Quarterback Dilemma 117

23 Light at the End of the Tunnel 121

24 History Repeats Itself 125

25 The Veer 129

26 Piecing It Together 133

27 Letting Us Run 137

28 Life's Hardest Lesson 143

29 A Tradition is Born 147

30 Now or Never 149

31 The Turning Point 153

32 "The Drive" 159

33 One Step Closer 167

34 Down But Not Out 171

35 Showdown in Durham 175

36 The Impossible Dream 181

37 From Dream to Reality 187

Epilogue 193

About the Author 195

Acknowledgments 197

PROLOGUE

The winter sessions of 1969 were every bit the torture our new coach intended. Sprints, down-ups, more sprints, and more down-ups. We knew the grain of the basketball court floorboards intimately. No rest. No sympathy. Just endless, repetitive drills until we were ready to lose our lunch, walk away, and tell the coach to go to hell.

That was precisely what he wanted. He was testing us to see what we were made of. He wanted men who would endure anything just for a chance to play.

What can be said about an underrated college football team that shocked its critics and won a title more than five decades ago that will mean anything to anyone today? Our memories of that 1970 season are as fresh today as what we ate for breakfast this morning. When we gather now, we pick up the conversation as if we've just left practice. We are twenty-year-old kids again, teammates determined to prove the naysayers wrong. Sportswriters had confidently predicted our mediocrity. That we played for a university better known for its golf and basketball programs did not help. We did not even qualify for the distinction of being considered underdogs.

"No Offense, No Defense, No Hope!"

The Summer 1970 "College Football Predictions" issues were neither encouraging nor kind:

- *Playboy:* "Wake Forest will be much stronger, although that isn't saying an awful lot remembering last season," one Wake Forest staff member remarked. "When we were bad, we were probably one of the worst teams in the nation, but when we were good, we approached mediocrity." Picked 8th in the ACC.

- *Smith and Street:* The 1969 Deacon contingent managed to win three games by 1, 2, and 6 points, and then lose 10 starters for the upcoming 1970 season. It's enough to drive a coach to dance except they don't dance at Wake Forest, a Baptist institution. Picked 8th in the ACC.

- *Game Plan Football:* The Deacons, last year, won three games by a total of 9 points and lost seven games by a total of 163, and they appear headed for more of the same this fall. Picked 6th in the ACC.

- *Kick-Off Magazine:* The Deacons haven't had a winning season in 10 years, but it's unlikely they'll turn the corner this trip. Picked 8th in the ACC.

- *Pro and College Football:* Wake Forest, young again, is over- scheduled. Picked 8th in the ACC.

These preseason forecasts by "the experts" described us as having no offense, no defense, and no hope. As if to confirm their prognostications, we began the season with a thorough pummeling at the hands of eventual national champions Nebraska. Undeterred, we shrugged it off and moved forward.

The 1970 season was a bumpy ride, punctuated by injuries, personal heartbreak, devastating losses, and self-doubt—enough to convince most teams pack it in. Indeed, no one would have blamed us if we had. But in the end, we surprised everyone.

When we meet now, gray-haired, softer around the middle, a bit slower to rise from our chairs, we honor each other, not with solemnity, but with grace and respect for what we accomplished together.

Few people remember that season, but we do. How could we not? It was our first real challenge, our first rude awakening to life's hard lessons. And it transformed us. Afterward, we moved on to life beyond the gridiron—*real* life and its vicissitudes—comforted and sustained by what we had gone through together.

The effort we put in to win that championship and the pride it gave us, became, over the years, like an old friend who is no longer around, but whose presence is still felt. In later years, wherever we were, we could lean on that championship and draw strength from our unforgettable season. Every player on that team could look back and know that doing something everyone told us we would never do holds lifelong benefits.

We wanted to win. Every team wants to win. Every player will tell you they are hungry to win. But only one man believed in his heart that we could, and *would*, achieve that goal. Our coach was an alchemist with the right formula, one that would mold and motivate us to do whatever was necessary in order to win.

Our miracle season came about during an extraordinary time U.S. history, a time of unprecedented social, civil, and political upheaval. Our path to the ACC championship intersected with a generation of young Americans challenging the status quo with their music, hairstyles, and fashion. Once staid college campuses became hotbeds of counterculture, where disaffected students rebelled against the establishment. Everything that formerly passed as acceptable was being questioned—from politics to religion to marriage.

Although cloistered from the chaos that occurred on campuses and elsewhere in the aftermath of such tragedies as the Kent State shootings and political assassinations, my teammates and I did not turn a blind eye to the daily headlines, far from it. We were young, healthy males, keenly conscious of the conflict in Vietnam and the struggles of our Black teammates. But we were football players first, teammates and protectors of each other. We bonded and became brothers on a single journey.

Everyone needs a touchstone. That season became ours. The 1970 Wake Forest Atlantic Coast Conference Championship and what we had to do to win it does mean something all these years later. Our failures, slow but gradual improvement, and victory in the face of seemingly insurmountable odds taught us life lessons still applicable today.

The season unfolded slowly, the first games affirming our critics' right to dismiss us. But they were wrong. Those early losses only served to solidify our individual resolve. And as the wins began to pile up, so did our confidence in ourselves and what we believed we could achieve. We had the ride of our young lives. And today, more than half a century later, the 1970 championship season continues to inspire us, each and every day.

"Champions aren't made on game day. They're made in the thousands of moments when no one is watching."

—Cal Stoll, Head Coach,
Wake Forest Demon Deacons, 1969–1972

CULTURE SHOCK

It was no accident that our championship team overflowed with players from New York, Connecticut, Massachusetts—and a whopping eighteen from Pennsylvania. From 1964 to 1968, Wake Forest Head Coach Bill Tate and his staff recruited heavily in the football-rich Northeast. They were well-schooled in seeking out good high school athletes overlooked by the big football factories.

The Northeast bred a different kind of football player—tough, gritty, and often underestimated. Tate sent a group of young, ambitious assistants out on the Wake Forest recruiting trail. Expert salesmen, they were adept at touting the benefits of attending a small school in the Deep South. Evidently, captaining my Ramapo Regional High School team senior year and being named All-Conference and All-Suburban at both offensive tackle and defensive end must have attracted Wake's attention.

Assistant Coach Beattie Feathers traveled to northern New Jersey to recruit me. He did not believe in the hard-sell approach, and for me, it worked. Though I didn't realize it at the time, our meeting in my family's home in

Franklin Lakes set the stage for a pivotal moment in my life. Feathers was not one of the "young" assistants. Already sixty-seven when I met him, "The Baid" had an accomplished past as both a player and a coach. An All-America running back for the University of Tennessee in 1933, he went on to play for the Chicago Bears, Brooklyn Dodgers, and Green Bay Packers. In his rookie season with the Bears, he became the first NFL player to gain more than 1,000 yards in a single season and still holds the record for all-time yards gained per attempt. During his tenure as head football coach at NC State from 1944 through 1951, Feathers led the Wolfpacks to its first ever Bowl game in 1946 following an 8-3 season. Four years later, NC State won its first game over a defending national champion when it beat Maryland 16-12 in a televised game. While sitting with my parents and me, however, the soft-spoken coach mentioned none of this.

Of Native American heritage, Feathers had sweeping black hair surren-dering to gray, a weather-beaten face, kind eyes, and a genuine smile. His soft drawl and slow, measured way of speaking announced his rural Virginia roots. He began by reviewing the academic advantages of attending Wake and shared glossy brochures of an idyllic campus nestled in the North Carolina hills. Then he expounded on the merits of playing Division I football in the Atlantic Coast Conference.

I knew very little about Wake Forest and even less of Beattie's football past. I knew only that this visitor in my living room was a warm, convincing speaker—the lack of artifice his most persuasive sales tool. "David," he said, his eyes holding mine with a sincerity that couldn't be manufactured, "If you come to Wake Forest, you will play tight end for us."

I'm not sure how he knew, but I had always wanted to play tight end, having last played the position as a freshman in high school. That this person who had just met me had somehow intuited this desire felt like destiny. I had other criteria as well for how I wanted to spend the next four years, the academic rigor of Wake Forest among them. Hearing Coach Feathers speak of the school's demanding program and the benefits of being one of only 3,000 students, along with its small classes and rich history, was appealing. I knew he was not merely spouting what he thought I wanted to hear. A master recruiter, he knew how to sell a small Southern college with a less-than-admirable football record to a wide-eyed kid from New Jersey.

Come here, and you will play was enough for me. Those six words changed the course of my life.

I had letters of interest from Syracuse in Upstate New York and Wagner College on nearby Staten Island. Syracuse, under legendary head coach Ben Schwartzwalder, was a national contender that year with All-America backs Larry Csonka and Floyd Little. However, after meeting Coach Feathers, the path forward seemed crystal clear. From that meeting on, I entertained no thoughts of attending any school other than Wake Forest.

If I needed other enticements, I missed them. I was unable to attend Wake Forest's February recruiting weekend, at which undecided football prospects were courted and entertained with parties and demure Southern "hostesses" who served as the visitors' "campus tour guides."

Instead, in the spring of my senior year I flew from Newark to Greensboro, met up with another future prospect, and took a taxi to Winston-Salem for my official visit. No planned tours and no parties featuring students of the opposite sex. Just the facts. But that was all I needed.

I was charmed by the picturesque campus set among the hills of Piedmont, North Carolina, ten miles outside Winston-Salem. Its 340 acres were donated by the R. J. Reynolds Tobacco family in 1956. A Jersey kid, I was surprised by the Southern accents and unabashed friendliness of passing strangers who never failed to stop and say, "Howdy y'all!"

The campus I visited was only ten years old, having been built more than a century after the school's original site on a former plantation in Wake Forest, about a hundred miles east of Winston-Salem. Its founding fathers were members of the North Carolina Baptist State Convention, whose aim was to educate young men for the ministry while also teaching practical skills necessary for livelihood, including agriculture. The Piedmont campus was beautiful and welcoming, perfect for a young guy leaving home for the first time. Any lingering doubts I might have had before my visit evaporated in the North Carolina sun. My heart was set on attending Wake Forest.

Still, when I first arrived as a freshman in August 1967, it felt as though I had stepped back in time. Only ten years earlier, Wake Forest had made the leap from a small Baptist college to fully accredited university, with aspirations to achieve national recognition in academics and sports. Chartered in 1834, the institution was struggling with its identity, one foot still solidly entrenched in the antebellum South.

Its Southern roots run deep. In 1862, the school was forced to close after most of its students and faculty left to serve in the Confederate Army. Vestiges of the Civil War, though far from overt, had slowed the wheels of progress.

With their minds set on transformation, the Trustees envisioned Wake Forest's other foot stepping boldly forward into a new, modern era, on a par with the "Little Ivies" of the Northeast—selective, prestigious institutions like Amherst, Williams, and Wesleyan. Determined to shed its stodgy Baptist image, it was reinventing itself by way of progressive offerings, revered athletics, and rigorous academic standards, not unlike ACC rival Duke.

Culture shock notwithstanding, I felt at home the instant I stepped on campus, as did my football classmates. For me, those first heady days marked the beginning of a lifelong love affair with the small university, my teammates, and the team we became.

I knew I was not in Jersey anymore, and that was fine with me. The thought of playing Division I football in front of large, boisterous crowds at old Bowman Gray Stadium was appealing. I didn't care that Bowman Gray was nothing more than a dilapidated former racetrack. The state-of-the-art Groves Stadium was under construction a mile from campus, and would prove to be the type of venue I had only dreamed of playing in.

I was also enticed by the relative smallness of the school. The freshman class I'd be joining consisted of only 700 students—500 men and 200 women—which meant access to professors and personal attention not typically found at a large, state university.

Despite everything it had going for it, Wake Forest was home to a few societal peculiarities. In time, I learned to accommodate them. I planned to attend graduate school, and, peculiar or not, Wake Forest was the perfect launching pad for my desire to continue my education and play big-time Division I football.

One social norm that immediately surprised me was the archaic attitude toward women. In June 1966, a group of activists seeking to end discrimination founded the National Organization for Women in Washington, D.C. The news and the new group's influence had not yet reached the Wake Forest campus, where patriarchal norms still reigned supreme. Dancing was not permitted on campus until 1965. The Dean of Women (indeed, there was such a thing!) doled out demerits to any female student caught kissing in public.

(Of course, the male kissers earned no such demerits.) In addition, women had strict curfews, were required to wear skirts to class, and even attended football games outfitted in heels, stockings, dresses, gloves, and hats.

There was another activity I found curious. It was mandatory for all students to attend Thursday morning services at Wait Chapel. Located at one end of the main quad, the chapel was the namesake of Wake Forest's first president, Samuel Wait, back when the school was still called Wake Forest Manual Labor Institute. Attendance was taken by the Kappa Alpha fraternity brothers, the Dean of Men's fraternity. The KA monitors took their duties very seriously. Any student caught reading a newspaper or book was immediately chastised.

Nor was Wake Forest a laboratory for social activism. College and university campuses beyond the boundaries of our sheltered existence were beginning to foment student sit-ins, marches, and protests over racial inequality and a growing military presence in Vietnam. The 1960s mantra of "sex, drugs, and rock-n-roll"—and the agitations that often accompanied them—happened elsewhere. Growing unease on campuses such as UC Berkeley, which led California gubernatorial candidate Ronald Reagan to describe protests as "rioting and anarchy" precipitated by "beatniks, radicals and filthy speech advocates," was read about in the news, not experienced. However, that was about to change in Winston-Salem.

When I arrived at Wake Forest for preseason training in the late summer of 1967, I knew things would be different from my days at Ramapo Regional High School. It did not take me long to learn how different. The football team ate in a cordoned-off section in a separate room off the main cafeteria, affectionately known as "The Pit." In addition to special seating, we also had a different menu. Our section of the dining hall was run by Annie Mae, a small, wiry, sixtyish Black woman who ruled the food line with a warm heart and a stainless-steel spoon.

We were "her boys," and she made sure we knew it. At meals I typically returned to the food line to ask Annie Mae for vinegar for my salad. Retrieving it, she would hand it to me, saying, in the sweetest southern drawl you can imagine, "Dodies, you never get them cancers, you keep on drinking the vinegars like that." Annie Mae was a trip, and we loved her. She was just one of several endearing characters at Wake Forest who made our home away from home feel more like a family.

As the sun set on my second day on campus, the first tangible indication of our team culture revealed itself. We were finishing up our Friday evening meal when teammate Bob Grant, a behemoth of an upperclassman, sprung effortlessly atop the table he'd been sitting at.

Directing his gaze toward the first-year players, Bob announced in a loud voice, "All you freshmen will have your heads shaved come Monday morning, or you answer to me." A 250-pound rock of a defensive lineman, Grant could press 300 pounds. He was not a guy we were about to say no to.

A black belt in karate and one of the first Black student-athletes to suit up for Wake Forest, Bob later played on the Baltimore Colts team that won Super Bowl V, defeating the Dallas Cowboys 16-13 on a Jim O'Brien field goal in the final seconds. As he pointed his finger at us, we immediately began planning our new looks. Some of the freshmen went back to their dorm rooms, grabbed cans of shaving cream and razors, and went to work, experimenting with various designs. The more sensible, me included, went early the next morning to the campus barber and got buzzed at no charge.

Not a single freshman waited until Monday to lose their hair. By lunch the next day—a Saturday—every freshman was as bald as a West Point plebe. At practice that afternoon we reported to Bob for inspection. All passed, our newly shorn heads identifying us as lowly Demon Deacon initiates. Unbeknownst to me, my second lesson in Wake Forest football brotherhood would prove far more dramatic than a simple buzzcut.

A couple of weeks later, before classes began but after more of the student body had arrived, we grunted and sweated through a tough afternoon practice in the blistering August heat. I could barely move and was beginning to grasp my new reality: In Division I college football, everyone was faster, bigger, and more football savvy. Whatever laurels I had rested on as a high school star were utterly moot. After practice, thoroughly exhausted, I trudged back to our dorm room, four floors above Kappa Alpha fraternity on the main quad.

The Kappa Alphas were quintessential Southern frat boys. It was rare to pass their quarters without hearing some version of "Dixie," the de facto anthem of the Confederacy and the tune their soldiers marched to, pulsing from its open windows, speakers facing out. They partied hard, yet, in the Southern tradition, took their responsibilities as gentlemen—or at least the outward appearance of being gentleman—very seriously. Their white shirts were always pressed, their manners impeccable (at least in public), and their dedication to Southern traditions unwavering.

I headed for my bunk and a well-earned nap, my roommate, Terry Kuharchek, nowhere in sight. Turns out he had taken a detour after practice to enjoy some cold refreshment at the Tavern on the Green, an informal bar next to a nine-hole golf course located a quarter mile from campus. When he returned to our suite an hour or so later, I could tell by his breath, slurred speech, and awkward movements he'd consumed more than a few.

Below us, Kappa Alpha was hosting what appeared to be a reenactment of a scene out of Gone with the Wind, complete with a bevy of Scarlett O'Haras. Young women milled about outside the fraternity dressed to the nines, complete with gloves and ornate hats. I'd never seen anything like it. In New Jersey, dressing so formally for anything other than a high school prom would have prompted astonished laughter and catcalls.

I was intrigued by this glimpse into a culture so different from my own. Terry, on the other hand, had grown up in a hardscrabble area of Western Pennsylvania, and did not view this overt display of Southern charm as an opportunity to embrace our new community. He saw it as a chance to yell non-chivalrous expletives and downright rude suggestions to the women below.

He began screaming insults from our window aimed at both the women and their hosts. Without going into detail, I will say his offerings were indelicate and profane. In any event, he got the attention of the Kappa Alpha brothers. They looked up at the open windows above, trying to pinpoint where the obscene jeers were coming from and shouting at the unseen culprit to shut up. Unintimidated, my roommate stuck his head further out the window and continued his verbal assault.

Not long after, we heard a clamor in the hallway. A rabid war party of Kappa Alphas was trying to bust their way in, pounding and crashing against the door to our suite. Emboldened by his inebriated state, my roommate opened it, ready to challenge the world. To this day, I am not sure what he was thinking—or, more accurately, not thinking.

As the three KA emissaries charged into the room, I absorbed another lesson in Southern culture: One does not insult the belles of Kappa Alpha. Southern manhood demands retribution, not that my roommate cared a whit. He continued his belligerent commentary even as the trio surged toward him.

I saw my life, new academic endeavors, and football future begin to dissolve before my eyes, all because my roommate couldn't hold his liquor or his tongue.

I watched, unable to move, as two of the three charged my roommate. Positioning themselves one on each side, they grabbed Terry's shoulders and began shaking him violently. Behind them stood Jimmy Clack, a 216-pound fire hydrant of muscle who played both linebacker and offensive tackle for Wake. Jimmy later started at offensive guard on two Super Bowl-winning Pittsburgh Steelers teams, an accomplishment that, given his size, speaks to his athleticism and total lack of fear.

Jimmy was absolutely livid: his face bright red, his fists clenched, literally frothing at the mouth. Just as he was about to step in and pound us to smithereens, his gaze moved from my face to my freshly shaved head. I detected a flash of recognition in his eyes. "Hey!" he asked, unclenching his fists and pointing at us, "Aren't you guys freshman football players?" Too terrified to speak, we sheepishly nodded yes, not knowing if that was a good or bad thing. Jimmy said nothing. Then he reached out with two enormous hands, pulled his minions off our bodies, and instructed them to leave us alone.

Out of context, there was no way Jimmy Clack could have identified us as football players. As freshmen, we played, practiced, and even dined at tables apart from the rest of the team. But because we sported the signature bald heads, he correctly identified us as fellow members of the Demon Deacons, and, therefore, brothers. Jimmy did not have to explain why he saved our sorry asses. His actions alone taught me the power of team identity and how it transcends all other differences and allegiances.

Jimmy turned to my drunken roommate—still chomping at the bit to take on the Kappa Alpha boys—and glared menacingly at him. Terry finally got the message and shut up.

The three mercenaries left our suite and returned to the party below. Terry and I remained intact. My Wake Forest career was safe, at least for now. I breathed a deep sigh of relief, grateful for the intervention and the lesson learned.

I'd been on campus only a short time, but had already learned much about Wake Forest, its Southern idiosyncrasies, and what lay in store. I was also beginning to understand the value of teammates, both my woefully outspoken roommate and the one who saved us. I grasped even then that the brotherhood among Deacon football players is stronger than anything that might jeopardize its cohesion.

Our journey had only just begun, but already I could feel the emergence of something special, a transformation that would define not just our college years, but the men we would someday become.

GOLD, BLACK, AND BROWN

Seventeen months later, two young men sat at a bar in Pittsburgh International Airport, unaware of the auspicious meeting about to occur. The taste of beer, the haze of cigarette smoke, and their carefree laughter created a brief feeling of holiday freedom—a freedom that would soon vanish.

The "International" in those days was debatable. Pittsburgh in late December 1968 was not exactly a coveted destination for travelers from abroad. Southwestern Pennsylvania, however, was fertile recruiting ground for college coaches: a hotbed of hard-nosed football players forged in the same industrial fires as the steel that built the city.

Passing through the airport on his way to North Carolina and his first Division I head coaching job, Cal Stoll deeply respected the toughness of football players raised among the coal mines and steel mills. The region had produced NFL greats like Mike Ditka, who left the Chicago Bears the year before to play for the Philadelphia Eagles; Johnny Unitas, three-time MVP for the Baltimore Colts; and Joe Namath, the young quarterback for the New York Jets.

Stoll was on his way to Wake Forest University in Winston-Salem, North Carolina, when he spotted the two young men and stepped into the airport cocktail lounge for a quick chat. Neither party recognized this chance meeting for what it truly was: the first interaction between two players and their soon-to-be-coach, a mentor who would transform them into champions.

Earlier that month, Stoll had been hired to replace Bill Tate, Wake Forest's head coach for the previous five years. A man of principle, Tate was the first to integrate college athletics in the South by recruiting two Black football players to Wake Forest in 1964. One of them, Bob Grant, was selected 50th overall in the 1968 NFL Draft by the Baltimore Colts and went on to play in two Super Bowls, earning a championship ring in Super Bowl V with a 16–13 victory over the Dallas Cowboys.

Tate himself had been a star running back and Rose Bowl MVP at the University of Illinois. He later joined the Marines and coached teams during his service, but his Wake Forest squads lacked the discipline to win consistently. He resigned in November 1968 after compiling an overall record of 17-32-1 from 1964 to 1968. The nail in the coffin was his final season record of 2-7-1.

Wins and losses aside, Tate and his staff had recruited an impressive 1967 WFU freshmen team, which, under Coach Stoll, would form the backbone of the 1970 Championship roster as seniors. This was Tate's lasting contribution—the raw materials that Stoll would mold into winners.

Faced with the unenviable task of rebuilding a team that had been the Atlantic Coast Conference doormat for years, Stoll had his own ideas about discipline. The two young men at the bar in Pittsburgh would learn about them soon enough.

As the first members of the 1969 Demon Deacons to meet their future coach, the duo was clueless to the fact that their brief libations at the bar before heading down to Winston-Salem would have real consequences. Burning lungs and bone-tired thighs would soon replace the memory of that carefree airport encounter. Stoll had deduced who the young men were but chose not to introduce himself. He struck up a short conversation, intentionally mentioning nothing about his position as their new coach.

The beer-drinkers earned the dubious distinction of being the first to join Stoll's "Dawn Patrol," an ignominious group called upon to serve penance for a long list of misdeeds Coach Stoll compiled with his usual meticulousness—

drinking and smoking in an airport bar among them. Dawn Patrol was Coach's euphemism for hard workouts to start the day. Weather was not an impediment. If skies were clear, that week's Dawn Patrol members would run laps around the cinder track as the North Carolina sun rose over the Wake Forest campus, morning dew soaking their shoes. Rainy days called for running up and down the steep stairwells of Reynolds Gymnasium.

The only variable in the routine was the mood of the assistant coach in charge. Some were more lenient than others, but Dawn Patrollers started classes each day exhausted, if not reformed. Under Cal Stoll's leadership, there would be no room for indiscipline.

Strolling through the Pittsburgh airport to catch his flight to North Carolina, Stoll was excited for the chance to test his mettle in his first-ever head coaching position. The small matter of inheriting a team that some critics considered bottom dwellers—not just in the Atlantic Coast Conference, but in the entire country—did not deter him. Where others saw defeat, Stoll saw raw potential poised to be unleashed.

While waiting for his flight to take off, Stoll was already strategizing how he would get his team ready for their September 13 opener against North Carolina State, his professional debut as a college head coach. For weeks he had been studying game films and assessing the skills of the players he was about to inherit. And he was not happy. The flickering black-and-white images had shown him a team that needed to be rebuilt from the ground up.

In early January 1969, Stoll called a meeting for three o'clock in a large, upstairs classroom in Reynolds Gymnasium. Built in 1956, the multipurpose brick edifice took its name from William Neal Reynolds, brother of R. J. Reynolds of tobacco fame. Complete with a pool, basketball courts, handball courts, weight room, football locker room, training room, and equipment room, it also housed the football, basketball, and baseball offices, as well as the athletic director's office.

Most players had heard over Christmas break that Bill Tate had resigned and a new coach hired. Most also knew that the new coach had been an assistant at Michigan State. As for Tate's departure, the players were only mildly curious. Everyone had expected Tate was on the way out and took the announcement of Stoll's hiring in stride. Little did we suspect how drastically things were about to change. That first encounter with the broad-chested, gray-haired Stoll would assure the entire team that the holidays were over.

Informed of the place and time of the meeting by Lewis "Doc" Martin, the team's trainer, the players strolled casually into the classroom and took seats. A blackboard at the front held what appeared to be charts displaying names and various colors, but no one looked too closely.

Stoll walked in at ten minutes to three, followed by three assistants. Once inside, he turned and locked the door just as two more players arrived. The room suddenly became deathly quiet.

Ignoring the knocks at the door, Stoll addressed the young men seated in the room, who now sat up straight, giving him their full attention. "Gentleman," he said, his stern gaze carrying more weight than any shouting could have, "I'm your new head football coach, and those players outside the door are no longer on the team." The knocks continued, growing louder. "You will always arrive at meetings and practices ten minutes early." He then advised us to set our watches and alarm clocks ten minutes ahead, an edict henceforth referred to as "Cal's time."

Stoll walked over to the door, opened it, and let the sheepish stragglers shuffle in. They had been granted a reprieve, this time. There would be no second chance. Stoll had made his point. From now on, discipline would be the foundation upon which everything else would be built.

Everyone's eyes then turned to the charts at the front of the room. Stoll stood silently, letting them study the display. They were depth charts developed by Stoll and his staff after watching hours of game film in the short time he had been coach. Each player saw his name listed by position, offense, and defense. Next to each name, a strip of paper in one of three colors had been taped. Some strips were either gold or black, the colors of the Demon Deacons; the third color was brown.

The symbolism wasn't lost on anyone: our school colors represented excellence, and brown represented something else. Stoll explained. He told his now-attentive audience that gold was a blue-chip player who would help the team win. We scanned the board for the very few gold strips, each man hoping to find one next to his name.

Black signified a promising player who, with the right coaching and the right attitude, maturity, discipline, and willingness to learn, would contribute to the team's upcoming efforts. There were maybe fifteen black strips, and more than seventy of us sitting in the room. Clearly, the odds were not in our favor.

Stoll paused briefly for effect. We stared at the charts, an overwhelming sea of brown. "And you all know what brown means," he said, allowing the implication to sink in. His introduction complete, Stoll announced that winter training would begin the next day. "I want to see what you are made of."

Coach's message was implicit. Those of us made of the "right stuff" would have what it takes to win. Improved fitness was only a side benefit of those daily, hours-long sessions awaiting us. He was looking beyond physical strength, endurance, and athleticism for something more profound—character, emotional resilience, and the will to push beyond self-imposed limits.

His methods would be severe—the results, undeniable. The bodies still standing after three months of Coach Stoll's "winter conditioning" and twenty, 4-hour "full-on contact" spring practices would form the backbone of our championship team. Each successive session separated more wheat from chaff, reaping a self-selected core of hardened athletes.

As my teammate Dick Bozoian later recalled, "Those of us that remained were determined not to let Stoll beat us down to the point of quitting. I guess it was a matter of pride."

Our daily routines became a blur of pain and exhaustion. Two weeks into Stoll's winter conditioning program we had been tested, stretched, and beaten down. Those who shrugged off the drills and continued developed a special bond we would carry with us for years. It went beyond camaraderie, the result of having been pushed to the brink yet refusing to break—a bond that laid the cornerstone for our success.

In the *Old Gold & Black*, the university's weekly newspaper, staff writer John Cooper explained that Stoll's coaching style centered around team pride and individual self-discipline. "Coach Stoll uses every means to build a solid foundation for a winning football tradition at Wake Forest. The entire process is long range, but significant changes are already taking place.

"Cal Stoll has a few team rules that his players must follow. He outlined only two, 'I tell a player to never do anything to embarrass himself or the football team and to be as good a player as he physically can.' The team rules may not be numerous, but they demand the maximum from every football player, for to give anything less is a sin, according to Coach Stoll."

Those few simple rules formed a doctrine that demanded excellence in every aspect of our lives, on *and off* the field. And for the next two years, they served as a beacon, guiding us through our evolution from cellar-dwellers to champions. The journey began in an airport bar, continued through dawn workouts, and eventually led us to heights that few believed possible. Cal Stoll had seen something in us we didn't yet see in ourselves. His vision rewrote the story of Demon Deacons football, one grueling practice at a time.

THE HEART OF
CAL STOLL

We learned early on that Cal Stoll expected effort and commitment, even when he seemed interested only in testing us to the extreme. The sixty-odd players who made it through his first winter conditioning drills in early 1969 bought into his coaching philosophy. In return, we knew he had our backs. At the time, our football skills were secondary concerns of his. He wanted players with "heart," a phrase he used often, and one that took on an ironic twist for him later in life.

A realist who made the best of what he had, Stoll was not one to lament his circumstances, and he expected nothing less from the young men he coached. Born in 1923 on a farm in southeastern North Dakota, just across the Minnesota border, Cal came from neither a time nor a place that would lead a young man to feel entitled. When he was growing up in rural Cass County, farmers were beset with problems few could do anything about, other than apply the only tools they had on hand: optimism and hope. His childhood imbued him with both.

America's entry into World War I in 1917 led to a demand for the wheat produced by North Dakota farmers. The government encouraged more production, but lowered the price when those farmers, including Cal's father, endured the ravages of a four-year drought. Crop yields were meager, grass scarce, and starved cattle had to be sold off for desperately needed cash.

By the time Cal was born, a brief period of post-war prosperity was waning, giving way to hard times for farmers ahead of the Great Depression, when prices dropped and farms failed. More than 65,000 North Dakotans moved out of state.

Football became a balm for Stoll. While in high school, he began playing fullback on a six-man team from nearby Tower City. He was not yet eighteen when he enlisted in the Navy on June 3, 1941, a day after his graduation and six months before Pearl Harbor. He served six years in the Navy, part of which was spent in the Pacific Theater. He also played football for Navy teams in Memphis and Seattle.

After his service, Stoll enrolled at the University of Minnesota on the G.I. Bill. Putting his football skills to use, he earned a spot—and later a scholarship—as a tight end on the Gophers football team, backing up future Minnesota Vikings coach Bud Grant. While still an undergraduate, he landed his first coaching job at Mound (now Mound Westonka) High School, where he helped lead the White Hawks to a Lake Conference co-championship with a 6-1 record.

After graduating from the University of Minnesota in 1950 with a bachelor's degree in education, Stoll embarked on an itinerant college coaching career. His path took him to assistant coaching positions at Utah State, the University of Denver, the University of Georgia, and, finally, a ten-year stint at Michigan State under the legendary Duffy Daugherty, who led his teams to back-to-back National Championships in 1965 and 1966. It was there that Stoll witnessed the most anticipated game in college football history firsthand, when the undefeated Spartans faced Ara Parseghian's undefeated Fighting Irish in East Lansing on November 19, 1966. The game ended in a 10-10 tie.

His pedigree established, Stoll landed his first head coaching job at Wake Forest in late 1968. We were part of Cal Stoll's arc, and it is safe to say every member of the 1970 team respected him and what he did for us. He made us winners when no one else gave us a fighting chance. From the "Old School" of football coaching, he was as strict as they come, while appearing unsympathetic to the trials he put us through. That was his price of admission. If we could show him—no matter what—that we would not flinch at what he threw at us, there were great rewards to be had.

When I look past his gruff exterior, I can see that Coach Stoll genuinely cared for us, not just on the gridiron, but in every aspect of our lives. But he also believed in tough love. The diametric opposite of a coddler, he had no respect for complainers. We who understood that indelible rule benefitted from his creed that flinchers don't win championships.

In 1972, Stoll left Wake Forest for what must have been his dream job at Minnesota. He compiled a 39-39 record through the 1978 season, during which he coached Tony Dungy and Marion Barber, among others. A 5-6 season in 1978 got him fired by Athletic Director Paul Giel, despite Minnesota's 1977 upset over top-ranked Michigan and a trip to the Hall of Fame Classic bowl. Being let go is part of a coaching—Stoll knew that. By then, he'd been at it for close to thirty years. Still, there were hard feelings at the time.

Hard feelings notwithstanding, Stoll did not hold a grudge. Three years after having fired him, Giel told a *Minneapolis Tribune* reporter, "After I had a heart attack in July 1981, Cal came to my hospital room. Suddenly, he was there. I was lying in bed. He gave me a hug, and he said to me, 'Some things are more important than any differences we had.'" That story that sums up Stoll's MO: Accept the things you can't control. Control the things you can.

After his Minnesota stint, Stoll did not wield a coach's whistle for seven years. In 1985, he moved to Italy to take the helm of the Warriors Bologna, an amateur team that captured Italian Bowl VI the following July. I doubt he learned Italian, but I am sure he had no problems translating his message: Work hard, be confident, and never, *ever* give up.

The Warriors were Cal Stoll's final coaching job. Ill health forced him to return to Minnesota, where he was diagnosed with idiopathic cardiomyopathy, a deterioration of heart muscle for which there was no cure. True to his character, Stoll neither flinched nor complained. He underwent a heart transplant in July 1987, back when the procedure was considered rare and complex.

Having cheated death, Stoll lived another thirteen years, long enough to see himself inducted into the Minnesota Football Coaches Association Hall of Fame and help found Second Chance for Life, a support group for heart transplant patients run by volunteers that attracted hundreds of people to workshops every year. In his honor, the Minnesota Football Coaches Association annually presents the Cal Stoll Award to an individual connected to football in Minnesota who has overcome adversity.

When he died on August 25, 2000, *The Minneapolis Tribune* reported this news. "Cal Stoll, who coached the Gophers football team from 1972 to 1978 but might have made a more significant impact in his post-football life, died Friday at Fairview University Medical Center at the age of 76. Stoll had been critically ill for more than a month as heart trouble caused damage to other vital organs. After liver and kidney failure, he was taken off life support at 5 p.m. Friday, more than thirteen years after receiving a heart transplant. 'He did a lot of things in those thirteen years,' said June Stoll, his wife of fifty-one years, whom he met as a student at the university."

In an aside I found so typical of Cal Stoll, his long career, and what he did at Wake Forest for us, the article noted, "What once might have seemed average, a 39-39 career record and one bowl appearance in seven years looked much better when his successors met with less success against lesser schedules." Indeed, Stoll was the last Gopher coach to have a .500 record.

Another article in the *Brainerd Dispatch* on Stoll's death quoted Ken Foxworth, a defensive end on Stoll's 1977 Minnesota team. I never met Ken, though I'm sure we could share Coach Stoll stories for hours. "The most important thing he did was give other people a chance to know hope was always there. That's what his legacy was as a man."

HEADS, HEARTS, AND DOWN-UPS

We were gutted.

None of us could avoid staring at the red EXIT sign above the double doors beyond the end line of the basketball court. Cal Stoll stood directly under it, whistle in hand, putting us through our fourth set of down-ups, the bane of college gridiron hopefuls. The sign's glow mocked us, promising escape just a few yards away.

Stoll whistled for another. With what little energy we had left, we silently cursed him, the fluorescent lights playing off the perspiration pooling on the varnished floor. For almost two months that EXIT sign taunted us, inviting us to walk off the court and through the double doors into the refreshingly cool North Carolina winter. So close, yet impossibly far.

We ran in place, elbows and knees pumping. The distant clock on the wall behind a backboard could not move fast enough to suit any one of us. I tried to push the thought of time from my mind, as if it would somehow pass more quickly if I ignored it. I wanted nothing more than to be out of there. We all did. But we willed ourselves to stay.

At the whistle we hit the deck for a quick push-up, then sprang back up and resumed running in place. That was the theory. In actuality, after flinging ourselves prostrate on the gym floor, it was all we could do to crawl back to our feet, only to begin all over again.

There was not a blocking sled or football in sight, nor would there be for the next two months. Coach Stoll was not interested in teaching football skills or strategies when we gathered nervously on the third floor of Reynolds Gymnasium in January 1969 for his first "open to all students" winter conditioning program.

NCAA rules prohibited formal team workouts in January, but Stoll nimbly sidestepped the rule by inviting the entire Wake Forest student body to attend his five-day-a-week, hour-and-a-half sessions. Only one student who was not a member of the football team accepted his invitation. For us, it was not an invitation, it was an order.

With his color depth charts at our first meeting fresh in our minds, Stoll had offered a not-too-subtle message. He was not impressed with our efforts during the 1968 season under Coach Tate, and wanted undeniable evidence that we cared about football and winning. His winter conditioning program would provide the answers.

We had ended the previous season 2-7-1 on November 23 with a 42-24 loss to Florida State. But the numbers tell only part of the story. We had beaten Maryland and put 48 points on the board in a win over hated rival North Carolina. We had come close to beating Virginia Tech and had tied Clemson. We lost to the number five team in the country, Purdue, by one point. The Boilermakers that year featured running back Leroy Keyes, who in 1967 led the nation in scoring and finished third in Heisman Trophy voting behind Gary Beban and O.J. Simpson.

We were scholarship athletes playing Division I football. Most of us had paid lip service to staying in shape in the offseason, or at least we had told ourselves we were in reasonably good shape. For Stoll, down-ups were a gut check, more about the state of our minds than our bodies.

Winter conditioning drills were not designed to disabuse us of our notion we were in reasonably good shape. That was not Stoll's plan. He was not out to show us our physical fitness was lacking. He wanted players who refused to buckle. Walking through the exit door in the middle of any one of those drills would have been easy. No one would have been surprised or critical, and many chose that route.

We hadn't grasped it yet, but those drills were Cal Stoll's rites to becoming a member of an exclusive club he would preside over with intense devotion. But first we had to pay the initiation fee. Those who paid would do anything for him and for each other. That was his goal.

Those of us who stayed had our reasons for pushing ourselves through those drills and the equally punishing spring practices that followed. Each of us felt the pain, but we loved the game to such an extent that we refused to accept failure. Reaching deep inside ourselves, we somehow summoned the strength to withstand any amount of physical and mental stress. It became a macabre chess match, Stoll pushing, and players refusing to show any sign of weakness. There may have been muttered asides as Coach kept his foot on the gas, but no whining to him or his assistants. Complaints would have been a red flag signaling that the complainer did not have what it takes to succeed.

There was also an unspoken subtext to staying on the team. The Vietnam War was at its height, and the need for more troops was pressing. As college students in January 1969, we were entitled to deferments that assured us we would not be conscripted into military service. On one level it made sense to stay in school, since leaving the team would have repercussions beyond not playing football. If we stayed, we'd be protected; at least that's what we believed. Come December, all that would change.

The gym's cavernous third floor was an open area that accommodated a full basketball court bracketed by two smaller courts that ran crosswise at each end. It became our Little Big Horn: We would either remain on the team and play for Wake Forest in the fall, or perish trying.

The largest group, players with the brown slips of paper next to their names on Stoll's depth chart, were the targets of Stoll's make-or-break process. As a member of that group, there were times I thought about quitting—everyone but a few stalwarts did—but I'd catch myself and keep going. I stuck with it because of my deep, abiding love for the game and as a matter of pride. I believe every player who made it to the end of those drills felt the same.

It was bad enough to see that our efforts over the previous two years playing for Wake Forest had failed to impress our new coach. We were stunned by Stoll's initial depth chart and color designations. We had done everything our previous coaches had asked of us. More than a few of us had come from winning traditions in high school and were top players in our respective states. Yet Stoll had deemed us expendable.

Cal Stoll was a different kind of coach. Once we got to know him, we had no doubt he spent Christmas Day before his arrival on campus watching game films. He was unlike any coach I had played for, in high school, under Wake Forest freshman team coach Bob Poppe, or Bill Tate in 1968. He was professional, no-nonsense, committed, and driven to win. He had the soul of a frustrated orator and was inclined to aphorisms. The more cynical players might roll their eyes, but the team, thirsty for some sign of hope and a light at the end of the long, winter tunnel, ate them up. As we gathered for that first winter workout one of his first statements to the team was, "You have to pound iron to make steel." We would hear that phrase repeated countless times in the months to come.

Stoll's workouts were devious in purpose. He had no intention of dropping anyone from the roster. He knew players without an intense desire to play would walk away on their own. He was fine with that. He wanted "winners."

A typical winter work-out session went like this. We'd spread across the main basketball court for warm-ups, with the familiar sit-ups, push-ups, jumping jacks, and stretches. Once those were completed, the first drill called for wind sprints.

In two long rows, staggered to accommodate seventy players, we lined up across the out-of-bounds line at one end of the basketball court. At the whistle, we ran to the near foul line and back. Next, we sprinted to the half-court line and back. Then to the far foul line and back. And finally, to the far end line and back. Slower players were passed and jostled. Then we'd repeat, Stoll and his assistants calling out to stragglers to keep pace. We usually did five repetitions, the original symmetry of the rows dissolving into a chaotic jumble of bodies.

Each sixty to ninety-minute session concluded with down-ups. Twenty-five down-ups were considered one set. We'd spread out on the full court again, accompanied by a cacophony of whistles and uncharitable verbal assaults from coaches as players began to tire. After four sets, we could barely lift our feet off the gym floor, and our pumping arms, which had exhibited strength during the first rep, hung limply by our sides.

The only change in this three-days-a-week routine was a unique exercise Stoll sporadically injected at the end of an already thoroughly exhausting

24

workout. Reynolds had eight squash/handball courts—high-walled white enclosures with observation windows looking down from a walkway above.

In this exercise, players competing for the same position were pitted against each other. A starter and his backup would enter the squash court and close the door. On the floor was an 18-inch dowel, 1-inch in diameter. On a whistle from above, both players grasped the dowel. At the second whistle, combatants wrestled for sole possession. It was a primal duel, made worse by the exhaustion wrought from the day's workouts. Spectators had a rare grace period to watch and cajole participants.

"I want to see who wants it more," Stoll told us, not maliciously, but with dead seriousness.

These Monday, Wednesday, Friday sessions continued into March, with Tuesdays and Thursdays spent in the weight room. Allowed to substitute squash or handball for lifting, I developed a lifelong love of handball that later shifted to racquetball.

Doing the same thing week after week became a form of mental torture. We knew what was coming yet could do nothing about it. There were no easy days or new, perhaps softer drills, nor did the weights become lighter as a reward for our perseverance.

By the time we climbed aboard the bus for our first game against North Carolina State in September 1969, our numbers had dwindled to fewer than fifty.

Throughout that long winter, discovering who was no longer among us became a ritual. Inside the first-floor Reynolds locker room, as we changed into our workout gear, we'd glance at the lockers. On many occasions we'd see that a piece of adhesive tape bearing a player's name was now gone. There was never an announcement, a posted list, or a daily tally—only empty lockers lacking adhesive-tape nametags. Each missing name told a story of someone who had reached their limit.

Soon after the winter drills ended, spring practice began. Those with nametags still affixed to lockers were not looking forward to the next level of Coach Stoll's hell. But we were ready for it. Little did we know what twenty days of four-hour Monday through Friday practice sessions with a simulated game at the end would be like. But we would face it as a team bound by something deeper than just the love of the game.

OLD-SCHOOL FOOTBALL

Oval Jaynes, an assistant coach for our 1970 team, had a football story, and Jaynes' story was not unique. All our assistants had football stories. Like the man who had hired them, they had played football in a different era, and in the changing social climate of the late 1960s and 1970s, even five years before was a different era. Cal Stoll and our assistants were old-school relics, carrying on a tradition that would soon fade into obsolescence—one whereby coaches were not questioned, players did not offer opinions, and injuries were rarely discussed if you wanted to play.

Jaynes had played end for Appalachian State from 1958 to 1961. In 2020, then in his eighties, he was interviewed by a reporter from *The Watauga Democrat*. In it he recalled a bygone era: "Things were quite a bit different then. You had to play both ways, offense and defense. You couldn't return to the game if you went out during a quarter. I played end on offense, and then I technically became a defensive end. You couldn't substitute a player as a specialist. Somebody among your eleven players on the field had to be the kicker on a kick. Somebody from that eleven who was on the field had to cover kicks, punts, kick field goals, kickoffs, and punt returns. There was no such thing as a special team player. Those eleven designated players had to do everything both ways."

In 1970, Cal Stoll and his coaching staff's hard-nosed, old-boy football discipline made everyone who stuck with it resilient. We never missed a minute of practice. No one looked for an out. If we couldn't play every minute of every game, we wished we could. Decades after our championship, in a retrospective article on our 1970 season, our star quarterback, Larry Russell, told a reporter from the *Winston-Salem Journal* what it meant to play for Cal Stoll. "He was tough. Cal would say you're like a blade of grass. You die a little and grow a little every day." Suffice it to say, Cal and his staff did not mind killing us on a daily basis.

I had my run-ins with Stoll's assistants. We all did. Despite a recruiter's assurance that I'd play tight end if I came to Wake Forest, in 1969 I found myself a second-team defensive end with an assistant coach who couldn't stand me. It had nothing to do with my play. The coach had an issue with the colorful tie-dyed, fringed scarf I wore around my neck everywhere I went. I'll admit it was a nod to the hippie culture of the times; however, as a political statement, it paled in comparison to Tommie Smith and Juan Carlos's silent protest on the medal stand at the 1968 Olympics to bring light to the racial discrimination and violence against Black people in the U.S.

For the assistant coach, a conservative, old-school traditionalist, my scarf was tantamount to burning my draft card or lighting up a joint between plays. To him, I was a hippie, a good-for-nothing softy who had no business being on any team he was associated with.

Our athletic trainer, the cantankerous but highly respected Doc Martin, was also a product of the old school. Head trainer at Wake Forest since 1958, Doc was an institution on campus. He prided himself in his thirteen years at Wake and tried to set an example for the athletes. Despite his gruff exterior, he was a sincerely warm and caring man. When I injured my back during preseason practice in 1970, he came to my aid, wrapping me in a brace, taking me to the hospital, and monitoring my progress. He was like a surrogate father to many of us, helping anyone who needed it.

Doc had one iron-clad stipulation, shared by every one of our assistant coaches. He needed to see we were putting forth the effort required. If he thought a player was slacking off, he'd remind him to pick up the pace with a quick snap of a buggy whip he carried with him, an action that would no doubt elicit lawsuits today. But we accepted Doc's eccentricities just as we accepted the demands of the assistant coaches.

We genuinely loved him, not only for how he literally "whipped" us into shape, but also, for his (even-for-the-time) outdated training-room protocol. He allowed no swearing or horseplay. Assisted by Jodie Puckett, the assistant trainer, we were taped, whirl-pooled, and patched up as if preparing for the Olympics.

Cal Stoll trusted his assistants implicitly. He valued their football knowledge, stamina to endure long hours and bad meals on the recruiting road, and their ability to convince high school football stars to come to a small school in the South with a mediocre record.

Trust is one thing. Accountability is another. Stoll's assistants were good at their jobs, but he held them accountable. After his first game as a head coach in 1969—a 22-21 surprise win over archrival North Carolina State in front of 37,000 rabid Wolfpack fans—we returned rapidly to earth. In our next game we were shellacked 57-0 by Auburn at Legion Field in Birmingham, making for a long, somber trip back home.

When we finally arrived back on campus, Coach told us to grab something to eat and be back in our team meeting room in Reynolds at midnight. Once we had gathered, he entertained us and his coaching staff until dawn with a film review. We sat in the darkened room, not only exhausted, but decidedly unenthused about reliving our deficiencies.

Coach ran a clip of each play, accompanied by a critique of each player's action. Then he'd pause the projector and ask, "Was this a winning play or a losing play?" Without waiting for an answer, he'd repeat the sequence and ask the question again.

We sat silently. There were no winning plays. That night, something very clear had been shown to us. To us, football players were at the bottom of the game's hierarchy, and our assistant coaches were authority figures, one step below our Supreme Leader, Coach Stoll. He included his assistant coaches in his assessment, which meant the responsibility for losses and poor play was shared by everyone. We were all in this together: Stoll, his staff, and the players.

Stoll once said to a reporter: "A champion is a champion because he does the things a failure does not want to do." Stoll's staff excelled at pushing us to do the things we did not especially want to do. They bought into his program and made sure we understood what was at stake.

Most of Stoll's assistants were in the early years of what would become long college coaching careers, which meant they too had something at stake. They aspired to advance in the coaching world beyond Wake Forest, preferably to future head coaching positions.

A college football coach is a nomad, comfortable uprooting his family and moving on, his worth based on the bounce of the ball, a dropped pass, a missed block—the vagaries that decide wins and losses. Win some games and move on to an assistant job at a bigger school with more visibility or a head coaching job at a smaller school they could use as a steppingstone.

At Wake Forest in 1970, the assistant coaches needed something by which to prove themselves, a noteworthy achievement to boldface on their resumes before climbing the next rung of the coaching ladder. Keen disciples of Cal Stoll's signature modus operandi and Stoll-isms, they were more than willing to stoke the fires as Cal Stoll pounded iron to make steel. When someone had to monitor Dawn Patrols, supervise down-ups, exhort us to keep moving in the fourth hour of a sweltering summer practice, or take note of our weaknesses, strengths, and attitudes, they were more than willing. Stoll and his staff were charter members of a mutual admiration society of which we were mere bystanders.

Winning was as important to each of those assistants as it was to Cal Stoll. They were just as upset by the inflammatory college football preview articles and their humiliating forecasts as we were, if not more so. Embarrassment on a national scale would not catalyze job offers. Those assistants would do whatever was needed, whatever Head Coach demanded, to make winning as essential for us as it was for them and their careers.

Reputations are built on winning. Wake Forest, Cal Stoll, and that 1970 championship garnered not a small amount of attention in the closely-knit coaching fraternity, opening up opportunities for those assistants to move on in their careers. Where they went and what they did after Wake Forest speaks volumes about Cal Stoll's system and why it worked.

Stoll told *Winston-Salem Journal* beat reporter Mary Garber that he admired assistant coach Ron Stark's "fiery attitude," an outlook we all shared. When Stoll left for Minnesota, Stark went with him, explaining in eleven short words what Stoll meant to him. "I came with the man, and I'm going with the man."

Nearly every assistant stayed in coaching for decades. Pushpins on a map marking the trail of their travels reveal as much about their love of coaching as they do about their professional success and the job titles they held.

Tom Moore, only thirty-one years old when he arrived with Stoll for the 1969 season, eventually left the college coaching ranks for the NFL in 1977 and continued to work as an offensive consultant for the Tampa Bay Buccaneers well into his eighties. His stellar career as an offensive coordinator included four Super Bowl rings won with the Steelers, Colts, and Buccaneers. As a quarterback specialist, two of his more well-known proteges were Peyton Manning and Tom Brady.

Another assistant became a head coach at Elon before moving on to an assistant job with the Oklahoma Outlaws of the new U.S. Football League, whose most prominent owner was a New York businessman named Donald Trump.

Tom Harper became the Deacons' new head coach after Stoll left for Minnesota and then went on to Clemson as an assistant on its unbeaten untied national championship team in 1981. Thirteen years later in South Carolina, a player from the Clemson team confirmed that Harper was still enforcing the fundamentals, just as he had at Wake Forest. "He seemed to be the one who could get all that I had out of me ... the one who could get the most out of all of us."

Over the course of their long careers, others took jobs at such reputable institutions as South Carolina, Gardner-Webb, Wyoming, Illinois, East Carolina, Michigan State, Vanderbilt, Iowa, Georgia Tech, Arkansas, and Georgia. East Carolina, Notre Dame, and Virginia Tech, as well as with the Miami Dolphins of the NFL and the Jacksonville Sharks of the World Football League. Oval Jaynes eventually became Director of Athletics at the University of Pittsburgh.

In his 2020 interview, Jaynes observed a phenomenon: a traceable coaching line that begins at Wake Forest in 1969—with a team of disrespected players in Winston-Salem, North Carolina. It speaks to the coaching expertise and knowledge passed on to future head football coaches, all of whom began as assistants under Cal Stoll.

Looking back, Jaynes recalled some of the notable college and NFL coaches he had played for or worked under: Mike McCarthy, head coach of Dallas and Green Bay; Jon Gruden, head coach of Tampa Bay and Las Vegas; Bud Carson, defensive coordinator for the Rams, Colts, Chiefs, and Jets; Chuck Pagano, head coach of the Indianapolis Colts; Urban Meyer, head coach at Ohio State and the University of Florida; and Skip Holtz, head coach at UConn, East Carolina, University of South Florida, and Louisiana Tech. All impressive coaches with impressive careers. He considered Coach Stoll right up there with them.

"I had some good mentors throughout my career," Jaynes said, "not the least of which was Cal Stoll."

THE INTANGIBLES

I t was a perennial problem. Bill Hildebrand had faced it. So had Bill Tate and Cal Stoll. Wake Forest had little ammunition in the recruiting wars against schools like ACC rival North Carolina, Notre Dame, Nebraska, or Penn State, all of which recruited and signed blue-chip high school players seduced by the chance to play in the national spotlight. Wake Forest was rarely in that spotlight.

As Dr. Thomas M. Elmore, Wake Forest Dean of Students, aptly phrased it, "The emphasis of the admissions in recruiting athletes differs within the ACC. Clemson recruits football players who are scholars, while Duke recruits scholars who are football players. Wake Forest is faced with the same problem." This recruiting disadvantage showed in our record books. Hildebrand coached the Demon Deacons football team from 1960 to 1962 to an overall record of 10-38. Bill Tate's 17-32-1 record did not swing the attention of television cameras and national reporters to Winston-Salem. Yet our coaches were not deterred by these statistics. Hildebrand, Tate, and Stoll had finely tuned instincts for recruiting good high school players from off-the-beaten-path high schools. They looked for athletes who had something to prove, young men with the mental toughness to dig down deep and keep playing, no matter what demands were put on them.

Chicago Bears running back Brian Piccolo, whose life story is celebrated in the 1971 film *Brian's Song*, was one such player. Despite an outstanding high school career in Fort Lauderdale, he was considered too small to play Division I football. The University of Florida, next-door neighbor University of Miami, and Florida State did not recruit him.

But Brian, with his grit, self-confidence, and unflappability, was precisely what Wake Forest needed. He had something to prove, and he did, becoming an All-American fullback and the leading ground gainer in the nation (1,044 yards, 111 points) as the Deacons rolled to a 5-5 season in 1964. A .500 record is not usually something to brag about, but it aroused pride in a school that had been dismissively referred to as "North Carolina's best high school" in the November 27, 1964, issue of *Time*.

Later, Tate and Piccolo were named the Atlantic Coast Conference's Coach and Player of the Year, respectively. Brian set four ACC and nine Wake Forest records, including most touchdowns and most rushing yardage. He was named Wake Football MVP twice and received the Arnold Palmer Athlete of the Year award once.

Our 1970 team was loaded with underrated players who'd been given short shrift by the major college teams—perceived as an inch too short, a step too slow, or lacking competitive experience—because they'd played for smaller high schools. We were recruited to Wake Forest because we were good athletes. Coach Stoll's rigid ideals, color-coded depth charts, and training methods that bordered on sadism did not make us better technically, they made us better mentally. His unrelenting drills in the searing North Carolina heat made us hard and unflinching. His whistle sent us into drills designed to break us—only they didn't. They built us up instead.

Inured to the rigors of Stoll's workouts, I was never awed by any of our opponents, and I know no one else was either. Our minds were set on winning, whether facing powerhouse Nebraska or an ACC rival.

Our star quarterback, Larry Russell, told a reporter years later, "I think we played with a chip on our shoulder. We weren't big physically, and maybe we weren't extremely talented or fast. But we did have skills and abilities. And we had toughness hammered into us by Cal Stoll and staff."

We possessed what coaches call "the intangibles"—things that can't be measured with a stopwatch, bench press, or measuring tape. Brian Piccolo had those intangibles, including the drive that comes from being marginalized. But even after his nation-leading year, the NFL overlooked Brian.

In 1964, the established National Football League found itself for the first time in a $5 million bidding war with the new American Football League for the best college players in the country. The NFL draft in November lasted a record twenty-seven high-stakes hours, with both leagues choosing most of the same players. Among the top picks that year were Dick Butkus, a linebacker from the University of Illinois; Joe Namath, a quarterback from the University of Alabama; and Gale Sayers, a running back from Kansas. All three were picked by both leagues.

In the South and the ACC, the media hype centered on Mike Curtis, a linebacker from Duke drafted by the Baltimore Colts. One newspaper summed up Piccolo's situation with the headline, "Nobody took Brian Piccolo, Wake Forest's hot-shot fullback." An Associated Press article run by *The Spartanburg Herald* in South Carolina ran a similar piece. "Piccolo's name did not appear on the player draft lists for any NFL or AFL team. The 198-pound Wake Forest fullback from Ft. Lauderdale, Fla., led the nation in rushing and scoring and had expressed interest in a professional football career but was considered too small by some for backfield duty."

Drafted by the Chicago Bears, Piccolo spent the 1965 season on the practice squad, while Sayers went on to become the NFL's Rookie of the Year. In 1967 the two became the league's first interracial roommates and formed an indelible bond after Piccolo helped Sayers recover both physically and mentally following a devastating knee injury.

Piccolo's intangibles, those indefinable qualities football coaches speak so highly of, came to the fore when he was diagnosed with a rare cancer after a routine physical. He fought the entire time, joked about his dire situation, and never gave up. In 1970, the George Halas Award (since renamed the NFL's Most Courageous Player Award) was presented to Gale Sayers for his comeback from a knee injury and subsequent surgery, which enabled him to lead the NFL in rushing in 1969. A month before accepting the honor, Sayers told the media they had chosen the wrong player. In words made famous by the film, Sayers said, "I love Brian Piccolo, and I'd like all of you to love him. When you hit your knees to pray tonight, please ask God to love him, too."

Piccolo died on June 16, 1970, at the age of twenty-six.

Football is a game. It is not life and death, despite the hyperbole used too often to describe it. Still, it requires the qualities Piccolo possessed—to never be intimidated into submission, but rather, move into it with courage, determination, and confidence.

We had all been inspired by Piccolo, as we were by any Wake Forest player who made it to the NFL. Few of us knew him personally, but we knew his story. It was a familiar Wake Forest tale. His death, shocking and sad, was in many ways abstract. We were nineteen- and twenty-year-old kids, unfamiliar with death and dying and its wrenching consequences. Like every other kid our age, we believed we were immortal.

We could all relate to Piccolo's aspirations. We were high school standouts who had been overlooked by the country's top teams. But until we could prove otherwise, we had no choice but to roll with it. Mary Garber of the *Winston-Salem Journal* on August 30, 1970, summed up our situation perfectly. "When a team leads off with Nebraska and follows with South Carolina, Florida State, and Virginia before even playing a home game, it can get tough." Then she asked Coach Stoll if the schedule was too tough. His typical Stollian response pulled no punches. "Our aim is to win the conference."

Garber's preview piece went on to cover precisely what Wake Forest was all about: underrated players who went into the season with complete faith that their coach was right. She wrote about our smaller-than-average offensive tackles, who would become crucial to the offensive system Stoll and his staff inserted early in the season. "This year, Wake Forest has Tom Martin, 6'1", 205 pounds, Gerry McGowan, 6'5", 245 pounds, and Vince Nedimyer, 6'1", 226 pounds. All are good blockers and are strong for their size."

She went on to describe the new backfield. "Gary Johnson and Ken Garrett will likely share the starting role at running back. Garrett is a junior college transfer who has never played in a college game. Larry Hopkins, who will be at fullback, is also a junior college transfer."

Garber, who had covered Wake Forest football for years, was an astute reporter. "Strong for our size" and "inexperienced" pretty much summed us up. And though she could not write it, she likely knew Stoll was right. There was something special about our team, something tape measures, scales, and stopwatches could not measure.

GLORY
HALLELUJAH

If playing in the National Football League is a useful yardstick for measuring college football programs and the players they produce, it's no stretch to say Wake Forest has performed well. By the time I arrived, the school boasted more than seventy football alumni who had suited up for the pros despite coming from the second smallest American college to compete in Division I. Although I was heartened to be a part of Wake's legacy, I was a realist and had no such ambitions to play pro ball. My only goals were to play, start, win, and graduate.

We all heard the stories of those who had come before us, and even crossed paths with a few. I had the unique opportunity to catch some passes in practice from former Deacon and four-time Pro Bowl quarterback Norm Snead, whose NFL career included stints with the Washington Redskins, Philadelphia Eagles, Minnesota Vikings, New York Giants, and San Francisco 49ers. During late-summer sessions, I received coaching from all-everything Minnesota Viking defensive end Carl Eller. Eller was a Winston-Salem native and happened to be a good friend of our coach. But that was as close to professional football as I was going to get, and I was fine with that. Still, I felt in good company. I played alongside Win Headley, Larry Hopkins, Larry Russell, and Ed Bradley, all of whom were talented enough to play pro ball.

The first Demon Deacon drafted into the NFL was 190-pound offensive guard Lou Trunzo, a third-round draft pick by the Brooklyn Dodgers in 1939. Trunzo carried nearly two hundred pounds on a rock-solid 5-foot, 6-inch frame, a fact that speaks to his ambition as much as his aggressive play.

Trunzo's story was a common one. Even more than eighty years ago, Wake Forest coaches sought out overlooked but promising players. Trunzo had played high school football in Saltsburg, Pennsylvania, forty miles northeast of Pittsburgh, during the height of the Great Depression. A college scholarship to a small school 400 miles from home must have been compelling for a small player with a chip on his very broad shoulders. Trunzo had something to prove, and a head coach named D.C. "Peahead" Walker gave him a context within which to prove it.

Trunzo started for the Demon Deacons for three years and obviously attracted attention. He played professionally until 1947, including a season with the Portsmouth Virginia Cubs in the American Football League, where he quarterbacked against teams from Norfolk, Richmond, Newport News, and Charlotte, among others.

Trunzo broke the ice and many followed. In the next two years, four more Wake Forest players were drafted by NFL teams, including Rupert Pate, a 6-foot, 1-inch offensive lineman and 1939 team captain from Goldsboro, North Carolina; Tony Gallovich, a 5-foot, 9-inch halfback from Vandergrift, Pennsylvania; and John Polansky, a 6-foot, 2-inch fullback from Buffalo, who led all major college teams in rushing with 882 yards in 1939.

As the reputation of Wake Forest talent spread, its program's pedigree became part of its allure for high school players on the fringe. The Demon Deacons did not win a lot of games, but they had coaches who knew how to pave a path to the NFL.

In 1967, when most of the 1970 team were playing freshman ball, the aforementioned Brian Piccolo was playing halfback for the Chicago Bears along with linebacker Bill George. George graduated from Wake Forest in 1951 and was a second-round pick for Chicago, where he won a championship in 1963. A product of the Pennsylvania pipeline, George developed a reputation for intercepting passes and wreaking havoc. He went on to be named All-Pro eight times. The *Sporting News* ranked him forty-ninth on its list of the "100 Greatest Players," and *Sports Illustrated* columnist Rick Rielly called George "the meanest Bear ever." In 1974, George was elected to the Pro Football Hall of Fame.

At the same time, former Demon Deacon Norm Snead was starting at quarterback for the Philadelphia Eagles. From Tidewater, Virginia, the 6-foot, 4-inch quarterback played safety on defense for Wake in the days of two-way football. His hands, seemingly twice the size of mine, could control the ball with amazing precision. The Washington Redskins drafted Snead in 1961 as its number one pick, second overall. Snead began playing for Wake Forest eleven years before I arrived and was still playing pro seven years after I graduated, a testament to his longevity and toughness.

By the time Cal Stoll was putting us through the grinder, it was well known the NFL had its eye on Wake Forest, even if we labored in relative obscurity. Contusions and sore muscles were a small price to pay for belonging to such a longstanding tradition. We embraced our small school's football legacy and felt we were a continuation of it.

Our chapter in Wake Forest history begins with Larry Hopkins. A junior transfer and one of the few Black students at Wake Forest, he gained nearly 1,000 yards in 1970 and, in two seasons, scored ten touchdowns and accumulated close to 2,000 yards rushing. Good enough to attract the attention of NFL scouts, he turned them down to attend medical school.

Larry "Russ" Russell, our 5-foot, 11-inch quarterback, gave up a promising baseball future at Stoll's request and became the keystone of our 1970 offense. Left-handed Russ, a First-Team All-ACC quarterback, was the player we'd see running extra 100-yard wind sprints after practices when the rest of us, totally spent, headed for the locker room.

We had linebacker Ed Bradley, who went on to win Super Bowl rings with the Pittsburgh Steelers. Ed played seven seasons in the NFL with the Steelers, Seahawks, and 49ers. In the 1975 Super Bowl, featuring the Steelers versus the Minnesota Vikings, celebrated linebacker Jack Lambert was injured. Ed, who had primarily played on special teams until then, stepped in, picked up defensive play-calling duties, and helped the Steelers go home with the win. When asked by a reporter after the game if he was nervous filling in for Lambert in the biggest game of the year, he replied, "Hell, if I could not play middle linebacker behind a front four of L.C. Greenwood, Joe Greene, Ernie Holmes, and Dwight White, I did not deserve to be playing in the NFL."

We had Win Headley, a 6-foot, 3-inch, 245-pound defensive tackle, who earned All-America recognition in 1970, was drafted by the Green Bay Packers, and played professionally in Canada for the Montreal Alouettes.

We had Ed Stetz, who, at 6 feet, 200 pounds, had 460 career tackles from 1969 to 1971, which in 2025 was still the most in Wake Forest history. A one-man tackling machine, he was twice named first-team All-ACC.

And we had Dick Bozoian, Vince Nedimyer, Terry Kuharchek, Steve Bowden, Ken Garrett, Gary Johnson, and a host of other players who proved pivotal in our 1970 championship season.

Wake Forest College won its first football game on October 18, 1888, beating University of North Carolina 3-2 at the State Fairgrounds in Raleigh. Five years later—despite American football's growing popularity—the college's trustees voted to abolish the game, feeling it was too dangerous. In 1904, according to *The Chicago Tribune*, 18 undergraduates died and 159 were seriously injured. These numbers seem incredible until you realize that rules were inconsistent across American colleges—not to mention laxly enforced—and helmets and shoulder pads were flimsy or non-existent.

Harvard President Charles Eliot went so far as to state that football was "more brutalizing than prizefighting, cockfighting, or bullfighting." But U.S. President Teddy Roosevelt, a Harvard alumnus and avid football fan, declared, "I believe in rough games and in rough, manly sports. I do not feel any sympathy for the person who gets battered about a good deal, so long as it is not fatal." Roosevelt, who wanted to play for Harvard but couldn't because of his near-sightedness, wrote of the game's benefits in a letter to a friend. "In doing your work in the great world, it is a safe plan to follow a rule I once heard on the football field: Don't flinch, don't fall, hit the line hard." Cal Stoll would have agreed.

The twenty-sixth president would have loved Cal Stoll. Cut from the same cloth, the two shared a similar perspective on the game they loved. I imagine Stoll never flinched at anything in his life. Our 1970 ACC Championship may have been the high point of his lengthy coaching career, but it wasn't the high point of his life, not by a long shot.

Roosevelt is credited with saving American football. A year after the calamitous 1904 season, he brought together representatives from several top football schools and called for reforms aimed at reducing on-field violence and injury. His efforts resulted in significant rule changes, such as banning the flying wedge and introducing the forward pass. In 1908, Wake Forest reestablished its football program, only to have its place in Wake Forest culture threatened again in 1955 when school president Dr. Harold Wayland Tribble, a Baptist minister, called for a deemphasis on athletics in general. His directive was met with protest from some 500 students carrying signs bearing messages such as "We'll hang Dr. Tribble up a sour apple tree."

Wake Forest football outlived Reverend Tribble and continued sending players to the NFL, but its coaches faced the ups and downs of small schools trying to attract the most talented high school players. When I was in school, the Wake Forest record for highest winning percentage in school history dated all the way back to the 1923 and 1924 seasons, when Head Coach Hank Garrity compiled a 19-7-1 record. Jim Weaver, who later became the ACC's first commissioner, coached the Demon Deacons football team from 1933 to 1936. His final record of 10-23-1 was far more typical.

The aforementioned Peahead Walker was a colorful character with a reputation as a smoker, drinker, and cusser. Known to cut corners in recruiting, he also doled out money to players and downplayed injuries. Yet, despite these transgressions, he was a very effective coach. His tenure lasted fourteen years—after which he resigned over a salary dispute. From 1937 to 1950 he amassed a 77-51-6 record, tied for Wake Forest's all-time best. Under his leadership, Wake Forest played in the first Gator Bowl in 1946 and the Dixie Bowl in 1949.

For me, and I imagine everyone else on the 1970 team, Wake's football history was water under a long-ago bridge, something to look back on during rare cases of boredom, but nothing to stare at. Yet somehow, that history became part of our DNA as players, even if we didn't consciously acknowledge it.

Wake Forest's storied past and its revered traditions provided comfort; they gave us a sense we were part of something larger than a single team in a single season. I doubt there were any football historians on our 1970 team; nonetheless, we remained acutely aware of the legacy we carried.

There are times when history, heritage, and tradition converge to inspire ordinary people to do extraordinary things. Stoll was a master motivator, and he unleashed the latent power of the past as we opened the 1969 season against North Carolina State in front of a raucous home crowd at Carter Stadium in Raleigh. We sat in the locker room before the game, listening to the rumble of the crowd and feeling the tremors caused by thousands of feet stomping in anticipation.

Rehearsals were over. We had made it through the barbaric winter trials and an equally trying spring. Stoll's preseason training, his constant exhortations to succeed, his inexorable pressure to make us give everything we had within us, all of it had come to a head.

We were conditioned to be fearless warriors, and we were in enemy territory. These circumstances alone elevated what Coach was about to do to another level. Heavily favored North Carolina State was waiting for us outside while ghosts of the past hovered in that Carter Stadium locker room. We were the Wake Forest football team, part of the same genealogical line that had given the NFL Brian Piccolo and Bill George and Norm Snead and, for God's sake, even Lou Trunzo. We were all part of it.

Stoll walked to the center of the room and began his pregame speech. His eyes were laser-focused as he scanned each face in the room. "You've worked hard," he began. "Now it's time to play hard. I know we can beat these guys. They put their pants on one leg at a time, just like us." Then we bowed our heads, led by Cal Stoll, who prayed to keep us all safe.

Coach then turned to an assistant standing beside a reel-to-reel tape recorder and nodded as another assistant turned down the lights. Softly at first, we heard the opening notes of "The Battle Hymn of the Republic." Stoll said nothing.

"Mine eyes have seen the glory of the coming of the Lord..." filled the room. As the first few bars wafted over us, helmeted players rose to their feet. The loudness of the music gradually intensified, and by the time the Glory Hallelujahs started bouncing off the walls at full volume, we were too. Any semblance of order evaporated.

The locker room dissolved into enraptured chaos as players roared, then head-butted and slammed into each other with the zeal of evangelicals at a revival meeting spiraling out of control.

"Now let's go out there and *WIN!*" Stoll shouted above the din. Caught up in the frenzy, senior lineman Ed George burst from the double locker room doors and onto the field, and we followed in a throbbing mass.

The ensuing issue of the *Old Gold & Black* noted, "The Wake Forest gridders drove 40 yards to pay dirt in the last three minutes of the game and were successful on the ensuing two-point conversion attempt to upset the heavily favored North Carolina State Wolfpack before 36,000 fans in Raleigh's Carter Stadium, winning 22-21 in an upset.

"Sparking the unbelievable and heart-stopping comeback were sophomore quarterback Larry Russell and senior halfback Buzz Leavitt. The duo combined on two key pass plays to set up the touchdown that came with five seconds left in the game and cut the State lead to a single digit. Coach Cal Stoll, in his first game as Wake Forest head coach, then elected to go for the win instead of the fairly certain tie. After the game, Stoll said that there was never any doubt in his mind. 'You play to win and not to lose.'"

It was a fairytale beginning to the Cal Stoll era. Caught up in that glorious victory, we weren't just a team that had won a game. We were the latest chapter in a story that stretched back to Lou Trunzo and before, underdogs who carried the Wake Forest tradition forward—one thrilling victory at a time.

IT STARTS WITH A WINNING ATTITUDE

If anyone on hand at the official press conference in a classroom inside the Reynolds Gymnasium on December 6, 1968, recognized the irony in the ceremony, they kept it to themselves.

University officials and reporters gathered at Reynolds to welcome Wake Forest's new head football coach. The recently hired Stoll, who would turn forty-five in less than a week, came with impressive credentials, having coached for a decade under Head Coach Duffy Daugherty at Michigan State. The new Wake Forest head coach had been brought in to turn things around. Many on hand that day had been in the same room five years earlier, when Bill Tate was assigned the very same task.

There was much to turn around. D. C. "Peahead" Walker was the last Wake Forest head coach to boast a winning percentage. Since then, the program had spiraled into mediocrity and worse. Bill Tate, who resigned in November, departed after four seasons with a disappointing 17-32 record. Before him, Bill Hildebrand left in 1963 with an even worse record of 7-33.

Athletic Director Gene Hooks told the gathering that he had received more than a hundred applications for the job, and that the selection committee had seriously considered "six or seven" candidates. But when he spoke of Stoll, Hooks' voice lifted with genuine enthusiasm. "Once we interviewed Cal Stoll, there was no question he was precisely the man we were looking for. We had some truly outstanding candidates. None of them, however, could match the host of fine qualities and experience Coach Stoll brings to Wake Forest."

Hook then shared a humorous aside: One applicant who was very much *not* considered was a gentleman from Great Britain who had written to the committee noting that while he had no experience, he was willing to take the job for free.

Under a new school policy, Hooks did not disclose the terms of Stoll's contract, stating only that it was for a period long enough to allow Stoll to establish a winning program, a benchmark he would reach in only his second season.

According to *The Winston-Salem Journal*, Stoll's salary ranged "from $15,000 up," the equivalent of close to $130,000 in 2024. For context, the highest-paid college football coach in America at that time was the University of Michigan's Bo Schembechler, who earned $135,127 in 1969.

Stoll's hiring was unanimously endorsed by the entire 19-member Wake Forest Athletic Council, comprised of faculty, alumni, and trustees—a sign of the universal hope he brought to a program desperate for success. "You have a big challenge, but you have great assets in some fine players, a campus ready for a winner, a ready-made football constituency, and a bonus in climate," Hooks told Stoll, a North Dakotan who had spent the last ten years in frigid East Lansing, Michigan. "We hope you will enjoy Wake Forest for many years to come."

Enjoyment was not likely on Cal Stoll's mind that afternoon. His work began long before the press conference. While the cameras flashed and reporters scribbled notes, Stoll's mind was deep in preparation. He had been poring over game films to compile the color charts he'd reveal to us at our first meeting three weeks later. The worn game films, along with his meticulous handwritten notes, were already stacked in his temporary office. He was interviewing and hiring his assistant coaches, making phone calls late into the night. Only Beattie Feathers, who convinced me to attend Wake Forest and play tight end, remained from Bill Tate's staff.

While managing a flurry of professional responsibilities, Stoll had to uproot his family from their longtime home, a task made more difficult by having a son who was a sophomore football player at Michigan State, and a daughter who was graduating from high school that spring and planned to attend Michigan State as well. In what little spare time they could muster, Cal and his wife, June, looked for a home to buy in Winston-Salem, driving through unfamiliar neighborhoods after long days of meetings, phone calls, and planning.

There was also the unstated but ever-present pressure to continue Wake Forest University's quest for national recognition beyond its reputation as a small Baptist college. A winning football team would draw attention to the university and its new identity. Wake Forest was changing, shedding its provincial reputation like an old skin, and nothing would show that more efficiently to a national audience than a winning football team.

Football was vital, not only to the university, but also to the surrounding community. A 1968 study found that five home football games generated $1 million in revenue for local businesses, equivalent to approximately $8.5 million in today's dollars. The study, I'm sure, did not include economic contributions by the players themselves. We did our best to bolster the local economy. Though we were forbidden to visit bars like the Tavern on the Green that attracted regular Wake Forest students, we were not strangers to other local establishments and purveyors of spirits.

Standing beside Gene Hooks on December 6, Cal Stoll's first concern was not economic impact. He was a man who left nothing to chance, and changing the football culture at Wake Forest was paramount. He knew he faced an enormous challenge in his first head coaching job. He had worked in the trenches as an assistant for decades, quietly observing, learning, and preparing. Now at Wake Forest, the glare of the spotlight shone directly on him. Stoll knew what was expected of him, and he had a plan.

Recruiting would be tough. Stoll knew that at the outset. As the new coach, he was reluctant to start turning over stones best left in their place, not the least of which was Wake Forest's high academic standards and rigid admissions policy that also applied to its athletes. The fine line between academic excellence and athleticism was a tightrope he would have to walk.

In a rare moment of candor, Stoll let *Winston-Salem Journal* sportswriter Mary Garber know that one of his biggest concerns was the difficulty in recruiting posed by Wake Forest's stringent admission standards. "Many of our opponents outside the Atlantic Coast Conference do not share those standards and, as a result, fare much better in the recruiting wars for top high school players. If Wake Forest were to compete on a national level, those standards would have to change."

He spoke of the challenge only briefly, perhaps sensing the minefield such comments represented. "The winning edge is so narrow that one or two players can make the difference," he continued. "The reason that the other conferences, rather than the ACC, have those players is clear. It's the rule that requires a minimum score of 800 on the college boards for an athletic grant-in-aid. We have got to do something."

Referring to a running back from Wilson High School in Winston-Salem who could not meet Wake Forest's academic standards, Stoll told a reporter, "There's not a better back in the East and maybe the whole country than that back at Wilson who runs like O.J. Simpson. I just hope he will go to a Big 10 school, and we don't ever have to face him." He told Garber he would request a review of that standard. If he did, his prayers went unanswered. The standards did not change.

Cal Stoll did what he always did after a setback. He moved on. He made the most of what he had, adapting his strategies to work around the constraints. In 1970, he would find and recruit transfer student Larry Hopkins. A dean's list chemistry major, Hopkins embodied the type of student-athlete Stoll learned to target—academically gifted and with the physical attributes to compete at the highest level.

Hopkins' arrival was still a year away that afternoon at Reynolds gymnasium, but Stoll was already laying the groundwork for finding players like him. In January, while he pounded us with his winter conditioning drills, Stoll told members of the Winston-Salem Kiwanis club that his first task was to develop "a winning attitude." Wake Forest had become somewhat accustomed to losing, so much so that it was almost to be expected.

Stoll's tactics, with his down-ups and never-ending sprints, were already recalibrating our attitudes. "Doing things right isn't a sometimes thing," Stoll told club members, his voice brimming with conviction. "Winning is a habit and so is losing. Winning is a state of mind and so is losing.

"I want boys with a winning attitude who will play every play as though it was their last," he added. He then hinted at what was to come. "We will follow my basic philosophy in spring football: First, we want to find out who wants to play, and second, we will find out who's willing to pay the price."

THE STOLL
ERA BEGINS

When Cal Stoll arrived at Wake Forest, he found himself in unfamiliar territory. No longer one of many nameless assistants surrounding the colorful Duffy Daugherty, he alone was the face of Wake Forest football.

To his benefit, Stoll had picked up a few tips for dealing with the media and the football-loving public from his Michigan State mentor. Credited with having coined the phrase, "A tie is like kissing your sister," Daugherty liked to inject a bit of wry humor into his press conferences with such statements as, "My only feeling about superstition is that it's unlucky to be behind at the end of a game."

Among Daugherty's many nuggets of wisdom, Stoll took one in particular to heart: "The difference between good and great is just a little extra effort." For better or worse, this saying became the guiding mantra of Stoll's coaching philosophy at Wake Forest.

While Stoll was putting us through our down-ups and sprints in Reynolds Gymnasium at the beginning of 1969, his grand scheme for transforming

Wake Forest football was already taking shape. His strategy included breaking us down first so he could remake us into a team far more cohesive and courageous than any one of us could have possibly imagined.

Confident he had started his master plan off on the correct foot, the rookie head coach stepped into his new public relations role in a typical all-or-nothing fashion. He set out in earnest to create a supportive fan base for the Demon Deacon football program—in Winston-Salem and beyond. His overarching goal was to put a fresh face on Wake Forest football and provide the fans with a winning team. He made himself available to reporters, especially *Winston-Salem Journal's* Mary Garber, whose stylus seemed to capture his every word. He spoke regularly at luncheon meetings of the Winston-Salem Kiwanis Club and the Wake Forest Sportsman's Club, his charisma on full display. He organized "Cal's Club," offering local youth prime seats at games, t-shirts, a membership card, and the chance to meet players. He even made his wife, June, available to a reporter for a feature story, humanizing the man who seemed anything but human during our physical training sessions.

Stoll continued to implement his PR strategy with enthusiasm. Drawing on Wake Forest's NFL connections, he invited famed Deacon alumni Brian Piccolo and Norm Snead to present a clinic at Reynolds Gymnasium for 150 area football coaches. These community-based efforts were strategic: Stoll wanted to strengthen his local support base, so critical to small college sports' teams.

Perhaps most surprising, he taught a weekly seminar on football for faculty wives, telling them at one session to "think of football as a game of chess. The players are in position on the field, and the coach decides which way they move. The difference is that you're dealing with human beings, many of them young and immature. The coach has to make an educated guess about how they'll respond or react."

When asked by one faculty wife what he does when his educated guesses don't work, Stoll resorted to satire. Folding his hands while devoutly bowing his head, he told the class, "Repeat after me: Our Father, who art in heaven."

Some eighty players gathered on Tuesday, April 8 for our first spring practice. The air still held a hint of coolness, but we knew the reprieve would be temporary. Ahead were four, three-hour sessions per week, followed by a walk-through on Friday and a scrimmage every Saturday until the annual spring game on May 10.

Practices began in the bright afternoon sun and ended at dusk, long shadows stretching across the practice field. That spring, Stoll dropped none of the demanding calisthenics from his hour-long winter drills. Jumping jacks, bear crawls, and endless running remained, but now they were prelude. He was not finished with his mission to purge the team of any player lacking the desire or never-say-die effort needed to win. We scrimmaged in some form every day. Not simulations, not walk-throughs—bone-jarring, full-contact scrimmages.

Not surprisingly, more players left. This was by design.

Stoll and his staff installed new offensive and defensive systems along with new attitudes. Practices were rigid and tightly choreographed, with players moving from one appointed drill to the next with the precision of a finely tuned instrument.

Stoll's stated agenda included establishing who our twenty-two best players were while avoiding "stacking"—the term for when two excellent players, a starter and his backup, occupy the same position. "This may mean moving some of the boys from one position to another, or even from offense to defense," he explained to the press, "but it will give the boy a chance to play."

Stoll knew that coming up with twenty-two starters from a group of eighty in one month—while continuing to test our willingness to play for him—was not a rote task to be calculated by stopwatches, tape measures, or bench press reps. This wasn't science or metrics. It would be best achieved by regular and constant hitting while Stoll introduced us to his offensive and defensive systems. We did not walk through plays. We ran them, offensive and defensive contenders doing their best to make the starting lineup. The lack of breaks to recuperate, both during and between practices, tested us to the highest level of human endurance.

"You can hear a good scrimmage, and you could hear that one today," Stoll told the *Journal's* Mary Garber after a regular Saturday practice scrimmage, the reporter detecting a hint of satisfaction in his voice. Garber agreed. In a short piece on the progress of the new-era Deacons, she wrote, "...indeed, even sitting halfway up in the stands you could hear the 'oof' when offense and defense met, and both sides were going hard."

Stoll's assistants mirrored their head coach's zeal, their voices hoarse from shouting encouragement and criticism in equal measure. One assistant, whistle in hand, was monitoring a goal-line scrimmage play when senior halfback Buzz Leavitt was stopped just short of the line.

The assistant dropped his whistle and raced over to Leavitt. "Never, never stop short," he screamed at Buzz, spittle flying from his mouth. "Keep trying, keep scratching and fighting to get in." It was a familiar scene, duplicated by assistants every afternoon, save for one thing. While the assistant was admonishing Leavitt, his teeth fell out, his entire denture plate landing in the turf.

His point made, and without missing a beat, he picked his choppers up, casually wiped them against his shirt, put them back in his mouth, and called for the play again. We now understood that even the coaches were giving everything they had to this transformation.

Without question, Stoll's full-contact spring practices were the most efficient method of selecting his starters. He had little time to gauge players' skills, but he could see the ones who hit or got hit and went back at it, who rose from the ground time after time despite the pain etched on their faces.

Inevitably, there was a downside to his method of natural selection. Players got hurt. Ankles twisted, muscles pulled, shoulders separated. Two potential starting quarterbacks—Ken Erickson and Dave Connors—went down for the duration of the spring practices, Connors for the rest of the season. Offensive guard Tom Jones had to have knee surgery. Most of us were walking wounded as we suited up for the annual spring game on May 10.

As spring practices progressed, more players left voluntarily. None of us who remained blamed them. We understood their decision, even as we chose to stay. The most dramatic departure, one that summarized our darkest unspoken feelings, came when, mid-scrimmage, a returning player vying for a starting position as a defensive lineman abruptly tore his helmet off and threw it violently down on the turf. Then, to no one in particular, he yelled at the top of his lungs, "Fuck this!" and stalked off the field. As we watched him walk away, no one made a sound; we knew what he was feeling. In silence, each man wondered if tomorrow would signal his own breaking point.

THE DRIVE-IN DEBACLE

When it came to physical conditioning, Cal Stoll had an ironclad belief: Players who are not fit cannot do what is necessary to win. The North Carolina heat and humidity only amplified his conviction that superior fitness would be our salvation.

He told a reporter from the *Charlotte Observer* he had a simple formula with which to rectify our team's shortcomings: He would work us hard. "A high percentage of good athletes don't extend themselves," he explained. "I always tell my players that they will pass out before they die. I've been in football a long time, and I've seen only two players pass out."

With those words, the die was cast. If we were smaller and slower than our upcoming ACC opponents in 1969, Stoll had it in his mind to level the playing field by making us physically fitter and mentally tougher than any player we faced. What we lacked in raw talent we would make up for with superior endurance.

Drills, unending calisthenics, and sprints also provided Stoll a chance to remind us who was in charge of the renovation project he had signed up for in December 1968. Every whistle-blow and barked command reinforced the hierarchy that would define our existence for the coming season.

The spring football drills that began in April 1969 made our winter drills and Dawn Patrols seem like aerobics classes for senior citizens. In addition to the prerequisite down-ups and sprints, he included frequent helmet-to-helmet contact. Stoll told *Old Gold & Black* associate sports editor Tom Jennings that among the seventy-six prospective players, there were nine junior lettermen, ten sophomore lettermen, and thirty freshmen who would be practicing. And that all of us would be worked hard. "From this group," Stoll said, "we will invite 65 to 70 to come out for football next fall.

"We have two objectives in spring ball," he continued, laying out his vision. "One is to get players ready and the other is to get a system ready." The two goals dovetail, he added. "We're looking for the best 22 players. We will test the players to find their skills. Then we'll fit a system around them."

We went through twenty sessions, the maximum allowed by NCAA rules. Each lasted around four hours, the sun tracking across the sky as he pushed our bodies to their limits. The sessions culminated with the annual spring game at Groves Stadium, an early sneak peek at the new and improved Deacon Demons.

Given the sheer ferocity of our spring workouts, we all looked forward to Saturday practices, not because they were easier, but because Sunday afternoon we took it relatively easy, something the Baptist founders of Wake Forest would have approved of. The anticipation of that blessed reprieve carried us through the worst of Saturday's punishment.

On Sundays, there was no contact, no push-ups, no jumping jacks, and none of the hated down-ups that left us gasping in the dirt. Workouts consisted of a short jog and a brief walk-through of plays. Then we enjoyed the rest of the day off. Some players might drop by the training room for a sauna or pump some iron in our closet-sized weight room, a place I avoided religiously, not in deference to Wake's founders, but because I was not a huge fan of weight training.

One spring Saturday, after a longer-than-normal practice, and with the thought of an easy Sunday ahead, I decided that an evening at The Thunderbird Drive-In Theatre on Konnoak Drive in Winston-Salem was in the offing. On this particular Saturday night, the drive-in was offering a Russ Meyer flick, a director known for what would later be termed B-list "sexploitation" movies.

Relatively mild by today's standards, they bore titles such as "Heavenly Bodies!" and "Faster, Pussycat!" Meyer's movies were short on plot, to say the least, but they were perfect for relaxing with friends on a Saturday night, especially following a tough week of practice.

After dinner, two teammates jumped in my car and we stopped by the local convenience store to pick up enough six-packs of Bud to amply lubricate our cinematic experience. Then we drove to the Thunderbird's entrance. I paid the $1 per car admission and looked for a parking spot. Only then did I realize I was far from the only one on the team with the novel idea to go to the drive-in. There, lined up in the Thunderbird's back row—with enough room between them and the other movie-goers to allow a sufficient buffer for making a ruckus—were a dozen or so more cars loaded with Demon Deacon football players.

By the time it got dark enough to begin that evening's feature, "Cherry, Harry & Raquel!", a tongue-in-cheek look at the evils of marijuana, the back row featured fifteen cars. It seems the entire team—drawn in by the titillating artistry of Russ Meyer—had shown up for the chance to blow off steam after a long week of practice. Needless to say, each carload had brought enough fermented refreshment to last through the evening.

We sat on the hoods of our cars and leaned back on the windshields, having turned the window speakers outward so as to make it easier to hear. No one around us seemed to mind, though the prospect of confronting a loud and lubricated group of Wake Forest football players might have been a deterrent.

For the Thunderbird's owner, the unexpected addition of fifteen Saturday night cars filled with Wake Forest football players must have been a bonanza. I suspect he meant well when he called Cal Stoll Sunday morning to express his excitement at hosting us, adding that the Wake Forest football team would be welcome back to the Thunderbird any time.

Sunday afternoon, we arrived at the jog and walk-through feeling as one might expect for a group of guys who'd imbibed gallons of alcoholic beverages the night before. We were not worried. Sunday's light session would be relatively easy even given our hungover state.

As we gathered around Coach to begin our jog, Stoll said only two things. The first was, "Did you enjoy the movie last night?" The second was, "We're going to do some sprints this afternoon. Line up on the goal line."

We knew Cal Stoll's hammer was about to come down. After we had lined up, Stoll blew his whistle, and we set out as fast as our leaden legs would carry us to the opposite goal line, 100 yards away. Queasy stomachs lurched at the sudden intrusion. Another whistle from Stoll indicated a quick turn round. We sprinted uneasily back to the start, the first beads of sweat forming on our foreheads in the humid North Carolina heat.

"That's one," he said. Assuming we understood the drill, Coach blew his whistle again. We turned and sprinted off again, our pounding headaches growing more severe with each stride.

By number five, players were slowing down, some reeling as the previous night's indulgence exacted its price. By number eight, more than one player had pulled to the sideline, hands on knees, vomiting profusely, the previous night's beers coming up as fast as they had gone down.

Coach stopped at ten. He said nothing. He didn't have to. We learned that day that physical conditioning isn't just about winning football games; it's about discipline, choices, and facing consequences. It's about becoming men who can be counted on, both on and off the field. The message was clear: In all aspects of your life, you must play to win.

Sprawled on the ground, we struggled to catch our breaths. Coach walked off the field, confident his unspoken message had been burned into our collective conscience more effectively than any Knute Rockne speech.

A NATION IN TURMOIL

Cal Stoll arrived at Wake Forest at the end of 1968—a year of riots, political turbulence, and mass civil unrest nationwide. In January, the U.S. Navy intelligence ship USS Pueblo was intercepted by North Korean patrol boats on January 23, 1968, while conducting surveillance in the Sea of Japan. One crew member was killed and eighty-two were held prisoner for eleven months. In February in Orangeburg, South Carolina, two hundred miles south of the Wake Forest campus, a civil rights protest by some 200 students at South Carolina State turned deadly. Highway patrolmen opened fire, killing three and wounding twenty-eight, marking the first time students were killed on a college campus.

In April, Martin Luther King's assassination set off riots in Chicago, D.C., Baltimore, and Kansas City. That same month, Columbia University students protested against racist policies and the university's ties to miliary research. They occupied buildings, including the president's office, and briefly held a dean hostage. Two months later, presidential candidate Senator Robert F. Kennedy was killed in Los Angeles after winning the California Democratic primary. In August, the 1968 Democratic Convention in Chicago was marked by violent protests and party upheaval.

Historic precedents continued in 1969, beginning with the disastrous Santa Barbara oil spill in January. In April, a band of armed militant Black students seized control of the main student union on the Cornell University campus, refusing to leave until their demands were met by the administration. In May, a mysterious illness, later confirmed as AIDS, claimed its first victim.

The late 1960s were nothing short of revolutionary, especially for adults under the age of thirty. Rebelling against the rigid and conservative trappings of their parents, young males and females alike dressed in bell bottoms and tie-dye shirts, grew their hair long, and rocked out to stereophonic recordings of Jimi Hendrix, the more decibels the better. Students held sit-ins, streaked naked through campus, incited riots, embraced psychedelics, and smoked pot openly.

If playing the game was our sole reason for existing, if we went about our off-field lives sealed in a vacuum, Cal Stoll would have been correct when he told *Charlotte News* sports editor Ronald Green there would be no protests if all young men played football.

In an interview published on August 15, 1969, Stoll told Green, "Football is the last laboratory of character available to a young man without going to war. Man is a competitive creature; most men seek competitive outlets, and football is the greatest of these."

"I'm not saying these people are right or wrong," Stoll said, referencing the anti-war protests. "I'm simply saying an athlete has a completely different sense of values."

These people. Our entire team was composed of "these people." We were young guys, part of a generation that had begun questioning values once held sacrosanct. Stoll was operating out of a completely different context. He had been to war. He had played and coached football for decades and was, without a doubt, a competitive individual. But from our point of view, he seemed either to be missing the point or ignoring it altogether. No one on our team could pretend not to be affected by the emotionally-charged events of the late 1960s, which, taken together, made it seem as if every institution in the country was being attacked by the very people our coach was referring to.

Whether we agreed with the protesters was moot. Americans our age were assailing norms that had led to the continuing conflict in Southeast Asia. Vietnam wasn't just taking up ink in the daily newspapers, it loomed over every one of us like a storm cloud. A lottery drawing, the first since 1942, was set for December 1, 1969. The student deferments we all had would no longer protect us. Instead, our fate rested on a random drawing for anyone born between January 1, 1944, and December 31, 1950. It was a lottery no one wanted to win.

Cal Stoll was well aware that college campuses were not the same as when he attended the University of Minnesota in the early 1950s. However, that knowledge did not change his attitude or his actions. A hard-nosed North Dakotan, his only goal was to create a winning team at Wake Forest. He never lectured us, never made political comments, never brought up the day's news. None of us knew his political bent, his religious beliefs, or his take on life outside of the game we shared a passion for. As far as his job was concerned, such things were irrelevant.

We, too, loved football, and even more, we loved what it did for us. We did not have to play; no one was forcing us. In many ways, football was a way to escape the surrounding turbulence. When we were on the field or at practice, nothing else mattered—not the war, not the riots and protests, not even the uncertainty of our futures. Comrades in arms on the gridiron, we had lives, beliefs, and philosophies outside of football that were rarely shared. Once we donned the Black and Gold uniform, we were one unified entity. All anyone cared about was whether you made the block or tackle or saw a hole big enough to gain a few extra yards.

Off the field, however, was a different story. Beyond the confines of Wake Forest football, each player had his own path in mind. Mine included grad school. Others had hopes for the NFL. But regardless, no one's plans included signing up for military service during wartime. Football could shelter us only so much. As young men of draftable age, we had to remove the blinders at some point and pay attention to what was going on beyond Cal Stoll's football laboratory.

But we lived in tumultuous times, times that had a way of seeping in through the cracks of even the most disciplined athletic program. The normally placid Wake Forest, cloistered as it was on its tree-lined campus, was not immune to the forces reshaping college campuses nationwide. The conflict in Vietnam was ever-present—in our minds, if not our daily lives. My freshman year, student activists erected 1,200 wooden crosses along campus streets bearing the names of North Carolinians killed in Vietnam, a number that increased to more than 1,620 by the war's end.

In December that same year, a history professor stood atop a large table in Reynalda Hall, the central gathering place on the main quad. A so-called "dove,"—as those who objected U.S. involvement in Southeast Asia came to be known—he was handing out anti-war pamphlets to a small group of students in an act of peaceful protest. Suddenly, to the astonishment of everyone present, one of my teammates, a sophomore named Eddie, leaped onto the table and shoved the professor to the floor, causing injury to his head and face. The campus police quickly arrived on the scene, and an ambulance transported the bloodied professor to Baptist Hospital. We never saw Eddie again. I'm not sure whether he was asked to leave or left on his own.

As shocking as this incident appeared to witnesses, it had a grave backstory, as we later discovered. Shortly before assaulting the professor, our teammate learned that his brother had been wounded by North Vietnamese gunfire. While we were reading news articles about Vietnam, the war had become personal to him in a way the rest of us could not even begin to imagine.

We did, however, suffer repercussions from Eddie's impulsiveness. Any football player who had a class with the injured professor became the object of his vengeance. I received my only 'D' on a blue book essay from him. Others on the team fared no better.

The following April, 540,000 American troops were in Vietnam. That number wasn't abstract; it represented people we knew. It was only a matter of time before each Wake Forest student knew someone personally who had been killed or wounded. And as those "someones" added up, the day would come when our student body could no longer keep out of the antiwar movement.

That day arrived on October 15, 1969, when the Wake Forest campus population joined coalitions across the country in a Moratorium to End the War in Vietnam. Some 1,600 students, including two members of our team, attended a service in Wait Chapel before marching to the on-campus residence of President Ralph Scales for a candlelight vigil. One of Stoll's assistants also showed up, not to stand in solidarity with the marchers, but to see if any football players had dared to participate. Spotting my two teammates, the coach told them, "Get your asses back to the dorm." His message was loud and clear: *If you don't leave right this minute, your scholarship to play football and attend Wake Forest will be history. Stay out of it.*

Scholarship or no scholarship, "staying out of it" was easier said than done. No number of down-ups or Dawn Patrols could block out the burgeoning discontent of a country in turmoil. Meanwhile, every letter we received from home contained news of another high school classmate being sent overseas.

Beyond the playing field, each individual navigated the roiling currents of the times in his own way. For one of our teammates, that meant tempting the wrath of Coach Stoll by daring to attend a music festival instead of practice. In mid-August 1969, while my teammates and I prepared for our opening game at North Carolina State, he joined 400,000 other revelers at the Woodstock Music and Art Fair. He showed up at Wake Forest three days after the start of summer practice. For having chosen rock and roll over football, he likely holds the record for the longest stretch of Dawn Patrols in the Cal Stoll era.

We were all just typical young men trying to find our place in a world that seemed to be falling apart before our eyes. Football gave us a structure, a purpose, and unity in a time when all three were in short supply. Cal Stoll's "laboratory of character" may have been more necessary than even he realized, not to shield us from the world, but to help us find our footing in it.

I considered myself lucky to be surrounded by a group of people who genuinely cared about me. I was also cognizant of the fact that students who did not have the safe harbor of a group of brothers in which to anchor themselves had a harder go of it. Many turned to drugs, either for recreation or as a means of self-medication. Some handled it okay, while for others, recreational drugs turned into a habit they could not live without. During my sophomore year, one of my suitemates, a freshman who had everything going for him, began dealing drugs. He soon flunked out. I saw him in town two years later, gaunt, strung out, with a new and garish scar running the length of his cheek. A shadow of his former self, he seemed not to recognize me.

Once, as a favor, for lack of a better word, I agreed to "babysit" two friends who wanted to "experience" the colors in Walt Disney's *Fantasia* while tripping on LSD. The three of us—a Wake Forest student, his girlfriend from town, and I—purchased tickets to a matinee showing at one of the local cinemas. I deposited the couple in the front row and went to the concession for drinks, popcorn, and candy, leaving my friends to settle into their seats and watch the previews.

When I returned from the refreshment counter a few minutes later, laden with beverages and snacks, I found them crouched on the floor, shaking and crying. Their eyes wide with terror, they gripped the cushions of their seats as if hanging on for dear life. Evidently the first preview had been much too violent and graphic for them in their altered state. Before the Disney feature even began, I discreetly ushered them out of the theater and drove them to another friend's house, so they could safely ride out the "trip."

A WORLD OF POSSIBILITY

The sixty-five of us who were left after Stoll's weeding out process—down from the more than eighty who had been on board in January—arrived on campus for the 1969 season ready for the task ahead. Having moved into our dorms on a Friday, we took our physicals on Saturday and then met for a team dinner in our cordoned-off section of the student dining hall. Stoll had left no opportunity for motivation untouched. We walked into the dining room under a sign strung across the top of the doorway:

"THROUGH THIS DOOR, ONLY POSITIVE THINKERS"

As we entered the cafeteria line, the mirror behind the evening's menu offerings held another sign in gold and black:

"HEY DEAC, YOU'RE LOOKING AT A WINNER"

The cognitive behavioral therapy was deliberate. Stoll's intention was to rebuild not just our bodies, but our entire concept of who we were and what we were capable of.

One thing had not changed. Our trainer, "Doc" Martin, watched over the food line like a nervous Brinks guard. Any player Doc felt was carrying a bit of extra padding was chastised. "Skim milk for you," he told one. "Put the ice cream back," he scolded another.

That first team dinner was enticing, I suppose, in much the same way as the last meal of a Death Row inmate about to make that final walk. As we feasted on steak, roasted potatoes, green peas, and salad, our minds never strayed far from the trials that awaited us. We sat by position as we ate—linebackers, ends, offensive and defensive backs—each group with their assistant coach at the head of the table in another of Stoll's team-building strategies. Laughter and camaraderie filled the room. An outside observer might reasonably think we were about to head out on an ocean cruise, not two weeks of two-a-day, two-hour, full-contact practices.

Linebacker Ed George captured the spirit of the evening for reporter Mary Garber. Referring to the work we had put in since Stoll's arrival, he started, "If we don't win now after all we've been through…" Then he hesitated. Overcome with emotion, he shook his head, unable to say more.

Stoll, on the other hand, was his usual optimistic self. "They look good," he told Garber, before quickly adding a caveat. "We'll be able to tell more Monday when we start."

When practice began on Monday, August 25, the thought that we could turn things around hardly seemed audacious. Cal Stoll's confidence in us, coupled with our own, was contagious. We were ready.

Monday arrived. We hit and got hit. We ran agility drills, then worked on specific plays in sessions monitored by the assistants, moving rapidly from one station to another. As always, there were sit-ups, down-ups, and wind sprints.

"The players came back in good shape, and I was pleased with their attitude and spirit on the first day," Stoll told Garber. "But almost everyone has a good attitude the first day," he added.

Stoll had narrowed his choices for the starting twenty-two. I felt frustrated that my goal to start at tight end had not yet materialized. But I was patient. I would bide my time and wait for something to open up. Others not designated to start felt the same.

That was the magic of what Stoll had put us through since January. We were a team. Whether it was because of our Coach, or to spite him and his color charts, drills, and full-contact scrimmages, did not matter. We were all in, bonded together by virtue of still being there, on the practice field, whether we were starters or not. The distinction between first and second string felt less important than that we had survived Stoll's program.

There was much to do. "Time is our biggest problem," Stoll told Garber. "I just hope we have enough time to get things done." For two solid weeks, the coaches put us through the wringer. We obliged by doing everything demanded of us, secure in the knowledge that if we took care of business now, whatever followed would take care of itself.

Even the freshmen were not spared. Many had been told during the recruiting process that their introduction to the rigors of college football would be gentle. "Coach Stoll does not believe in using freshmen as sacrificial lambs" was part of the pitch given to innocent and uninitiated high school seniors. But as more upperclassmen landed on the injured reserve list, incoming players were asked to report early. There were not enough bodies for the drills, and Coach needed to put the finishing touches on his plans before our opener against North Carolina State.

Our belief in ourselves was at an all-time high, but if we needed more inspiration outside of Cal Stoll's fervor and optimism, we got it from two unrelated incidents that summer. Four weeks before we began preseason practice in earnest, American astronaut Neil Armstrong stepped from Apollo 11's lunar module, Eagle, onto the moon's surface. A television camera mounted on its side broadcast Armstrong's first steps to millions of viewers worldwide. The landing fulfilled a promise made by President John F. Kennedy in 1961 that Americans would accomplish the job by the end of the decade.

On July 21st, when Armstrong famously said, "One small step for man; one giant leap for mankind," he made anything seem possible. The crackling transmission of his voice broadcast from the moon into our living rooms carried not just his words, but a profound sense of possibility that resonated deeply inside every person watching. Americans throughout the country were exuberant, and we were no exception.

The second event occurred the weekend after preseason practices began, when the 1969 Super Bowl Champion New York Jets—led by their outspoken QB Joe Namath—came to town. In one of his strategic PR stunts, Stoll had invited the Jets to Winston-Salem to play the Minnesota Vikings in an exhibition game under newly christened Groves Stadium. The Vikings, with Winston-Salem native and Cal Stoll friend Carl Eller at defensive end, had lost to the Jets Super Bowl opponents, the Baltimore Colts, in the division title game.

Namath was an icon. Many of my teammates from Pennsylvania knew where he'd come from and what he represented: hard-nosed football, the brand of football we aspired to. Before the Super Bowl, the Jets had been huge underdogs. The Colts, with the league's second most potent offense and its best defense, were 18-point favorites. Namath was unfazed. At a press conference he famously announced, "The Jets will win Sunday. I guarantee it."

Broadway Joe's bravado proved prescient. The son of a steelworker from Beaver Falls, Pennsylvania led his underrated team to a 16-7 win. We hoped, perhaps unconsciously, that Namath's seemingly supernatural presence on our field would transfer some of that underdog magic onto us.

In what was billed as a "Meet the Deacons Night," we opened the spectacle with an intrasquad scrimmage. As Stoll had envisioned, the event drew a good crowd—though it was no secret who they had come to see. While we scrimmaged, the charismatic Namath sat patiently through several radio and television interviews, then trotted out onto the field in his signature white cleats and trademark Fu Manchu mustache to the cheers of 10,000 adoring fans.

As we sat in front-row seats at Groves, watching the pros play, the message was clear. We could win. We *would* win. Just like the underdog Jets, just like the miraculous moon-landing, we would bring our dream to fruition.

A TEAM WITH HEART

After our dramatic win over NC State in our first contest, the 1969 season featured few "Glory Hallelujahs." Undaunted by the losses, we stood firm and grew, transformed by the very trials meant to break us. Our efforts didn't yield many victories, but they made impact. Like seeds planted in fertile soil, they were waiting for the right conditions to sprout.

Everyone could see things starting to come together. Through the pain and the agony, through the attrition and injuries, through the hell that Cal Stoll put us through, something was taking shape. Something that would change the narrative of Wake Forest football.

Stoll's prayer, "Our Father who art in heaven," had been answered, though not in the way any of us expected. Redemption would come, not from divine sources, but through the blood, sweat, and tears of those willing to pay the price.

Coach convinced us we were capable of better. He chose not to dwell on the strengths of the teams that beat us, but rather, on our habit of beating ourselves. He knew we were up against superior players in many of our contests, but he never vacillated in his assertion we had the tools to win.

Game films don't lie. A bounce here, an opening there, and we could have won the game.

When speaking to reporters about the mismatches we faced, butting heads against teams that were bigger, faster, and deeper, he quipped, "We have changed our colors from gold and black to black and blue." His joke may have drawn sympathetic chuckles from the press, but there was no denying the truth behind his humor. We were undisputed underdogs.

Even so, there were highlights. We had two come-from-behind, last-minute wins. After one, the locker room became the scene of such raucous celebrating that a reporter complained he was unable to ask Stoll questions over the noise.

And, of course, there were lowlights. Against Duke we managed to turn the ball over ten times, committing six fumbles and four interceptions.

Finally, there were no lights: degrading losses to Auburn and the University of Miami that bruised more than our bodies.

"We're not that bad," Stoll told reporters at a post-game press conference after Auburn humiliated us 57-0. "They're seasoned, experienced, and big. They outweighed us 20 to 30 pounds per man," he added, acknowledging the physical mismatch without surrendering to it. "Wake Forest will pick up the pieces and start fighting again; the season isn't over."

When it was Wake Forest Sports Information Director Dick Barkley's turn to speak, he injected a bit of dark humor. "On the way from Auburn to the Montgomery airport, I fell asleep and dreamed Auburn scored again."

We ended the season with a 3-7 record—seventh place in the ACC, above cellar dweller University of Virginia. In his talk to the Sportsman's Club before the Maryland game, Stoll emphasized the positive, reinforcing who we were beyond our win-loss record. "We have some good kids. We may not be as skilled or as big or as fast as some of the other teams, but I don't know anyone who has a corner on us in heart."

After each loss, he urged us to go all out, no matter what was happening on the field. Before suiting up to face Virginia Tech, he told us to "show them what an alley fight really is." We did, winning 16-10.

We won two other games in alley-fight fashion. A last-minute, come-from-behind win against North Carolina State left us jumping for joy. And against Virigina, after falling behind by two touchdowns in the fourth quarter, we regrouped, sealing the victory in the last minute with a two-point safety.

In the Virginia game, players asserted themselves with a passion. Linebacker Ed Bradley was a virtual battering ram, making nine tackles. Win Headley added eight more, throwing himself into the fray with reckless courage. Quarterback Larry Russell was an offensive juggernaut, leading the team in both passing and rushing. Tight end Gary Winrow led all receivers, his hands steady even when those of others faltered. On defense, Terry Kuharchek led the team in interceptions, while Ed Stetz was a ferocious tackler.

After the nailbiter against Virginia, Stoll told the press, "We had heard and read in the papers that we were too small and couldn't hit. We took the challenge and did something about it today."

Our inconsistent play throughout that 1969 season was a source of frustration. We learned how difficult it is to grab whatever momentum we had and build on it. For every great catch, tackle, or interception that portrayed excellence, there was a momentary lapse of competence.

This cycle of elation and despair began early. Our opening upset against North Carolina State in front of 40,000 Wolfpack fans was followed by a humiliating defeat at the hands of Auburn. Our second win of the season at home against Virginia Tech preceded consecutive losses to Duke, Clemson, and North Carolina.

The seesaw pattern continued, inexorable and maddening. Our exciting win over Virginia to stay out of last place was followed by a loss to undefeated ACC champion South Carolina and a drubbing from Miami. For us, it became a vicious cycle with no discernable way out. But for Stoll, our ups and downs signified nothing more than growing pains. Coach knew that once our team identity was established and ingrained into each of us, we would rewrite Wake Forest's football legacy.

Within those seven losses, however, there were signs that we possessed talented, capable players who seized opportunity, making good plays that briefly turned things around. It obviously wasn't enough, but it showed us we could compete. Clarity came in spurts, fleeting stretches when everything clicked and we caught a glimpse of what we could become.

During the 1969 season, names emerged in newspaper clippings covering our efforts. The announcements were not in banner headlines because, despite Cal Stoll's efforts, we continued Wake Forest's losing tradition. But individual players had done things that would, in 1970, turn the tide: Larry Russell, Gary Johnson, Steve Bowden, Gary Winrow, Vince Nedimyer, Gary German,

Win Headley, Ed Stetz, Ed Bradley, Dick Bozoian, Terry Kuharchek, and Gerry McGowan. A good block, a darting run, an outstanding tackle, a great catch, an interception. I read the clippings now, yellowed with age, but preserving the first signs of what was to come.

Our non-conference rivals—Auburn, Virginia Tech, and Miami—had the upper hand. They were football factories, unrestricted by the high academic standards Wake Forest imposed on its recruits. But even discounting those losses, we did almost as poorly against our ACC rivals.

After our loss to ACC opponent Clemson, who finished fourth that year, Tigers head Coach Frank Howard made note of the imbalance. "The entrance requirements of the ACC mean that the conference is playing with brilliant students against football players. When we set up those academic require-ments, they said we would lead the nation in academics, and I told them it would lead to something else—losses. We can't get those knuckleheads in like the Southeastern Conference and the Big 10," he told the press.

That was a coach's lament. As players, we did not care whom we played nor the SAT scores of the kid who had just run over us. We would have taken on the Super Bowl champion New York Jets if they were on the schedule. Our pride demanded nothing less.

To add salt to our wounds, only one of our three victories came at home, not a trend to endear us to our beleaguered fan base, who sat through rain and cold to support us.

Our final loss to Miami in the old Orange Bowl stadium in front of 25,000 Hurricanes fans was the final straw—the one that broke us. It had been a long, taxing season. After our 49-7 drubbing, the Miami press described the encounter as a mild workout for Miami, noting that Wake Forest was "unques-tionably the weakest to appear in a college game in this arena."

Inside our visiting team locker room, there were tears. Overcome with emotion, we did not have the energy to pull off our uniforms for a final time and shower. Frustrated, tired, far from home and from the hope we'd had in September, we felt wholly and utterly dejected. Our season was over, and we had not redeemed ourselves the way we'd imagined after working so hard.

But in addition to the tears, there was anger. Anger that we did not perform the way we knew we could. Anger that all the work we'd put in for the previous eleven months had been capped with a disastrous season-ending loss.

Anger can be a good motivator at times. It provides focus. It engenders a determination not to suffer the jokes and sports-writing cliches poking fun at our ineptitude. We knew we were better than that. Deep inside each of us, we absolutely knew it. But the season was over, and there was nothing we could do other than prepare for next year with a vengeance.

I have no doubt our lackluster 1969 season led to the negative 'sports prediction headlines' leading into the 1970 season, the writers of which were lazy and flip. They had not checked in with the Demon Deacons' players who were overcome with grief after our drubbing at the hands of Miami. Had they bothered to, the *Playboy* article author might have changed his headline to "Pissed Off and Determined."

At the press conference following the game, quarterback Ken Erickson, who had played in place of the injured Larry Russell, spoke for all of us when he said, "Don't judge us on this game. Wake Forest will be playing in a bowl game one of these years soon."

The Associated Press reporter who was on hand must have heard something in Ken's voice when he made that statement. "Erickson and 41 other players who saw action Friday night as the Deacons ended their 1969 season with a 49-7 loss to Miami and a 3-7 record must really believe that," he wrote. "Either they must, or they should all turn to acting, because a team is not expected to be crying in the dressing room after its seventh loss. Maybe it is because Coach Cal Stoll is a man with faith and understanding."

Then he nailed it; he knew why we were crying. "The Deacs cried because they are a team with heart."

If I needed any further motivation after the Miami game, it would come soon enough. After I showered and changed, I left the locker room to board our bus to Miami International and the long flight home. Drained from the loss, the long season, and my frustrations about wanting to play more, my mind was a million miles away.

Walking out of the stadium toward the parking lot, I saw a group of Miami students lingering outside. I recognized one of them, a former teammate from Ramapo Regional High School, where I had captained the football team and, therefore, was, in that small world, what some people called a Big Man on Campus. He was not a friend, but had apparently felt slighted for years, having played in high school but evidently never getting the accolades he thought he deserved. He must have been waiting for this chance all season.

"Big Dave Doda, the star," he said, elated at the chance to give me a comeuppance I was not aware I needed. "You guys did great today. Really looked good," he shouted, as his friends laughed. "You're still a star, Doda. Well, done."

I could have said something, but it didn't seem worth it. I stared back at him briefly before boarding the bus.

Next year, my friend, I thought. *Next year will be different.*

BREAKING BARRIERS WITH A PEN

ary Garber did her own down-ups, or at least the metaphorical equivalent. She did them alone and never flinched. In the scorching heat of summer practices and the biting cold of late-season games, she was there, a constant presence on the sidelines, notebook in hand, her small frame almost lost among the hulking players and coaches.

She was a groundbreaker, a female in a male-dominated occupation who humbly went about her business, propelled not by the equal rights women were beginning to demand in the '60s, but by her desire to write about things she valued.

A pioneering and tenacious award-winning journalist, Garber had fought hard to establish herself as a sportswriter. Yet the majority of us were oblivious to the battles she had waged to stand on those sidelines. We never could have predicted that the woman who covered the daily ins and outs of Wake Forest football would be inducted into the National Sportscasters and Sportswriters Association Hall of Fame. We knew only that Mary Garber was a writer who prompted people to buy newspapers anticipating what she had to say. We also knew that we froze when an assistant coach pulled us aside and said, "Mary Garber would like a word with you," sending jolts of terror through even our toughest players.

She had that effect. Even the most garilous among us was petrified to speak to a reporter who would announce our feelings to the world, or at least to the readers of the *Winston-Salem Journal*. And we knew that no matter how tongue-tied we were speaking to Garber, her skillfully written articles would make sense to readers. We knew that because it was pretty obvious. But none of us realized how fortunate we were to have someone with her talent and expertise telling our stories.

Most women in journalism in the 1940s, '50s, and into the '60s covered primarily "soft news"—social-page pieces or weekend supplements featuring new neighbors, wedding announcements, cooking columns, and childcare advice. Their bylines rarely appeared in the sports section where the "real action" was happening.

Garber had paid her dues writing such inconsequential columns, but she was a card-carrying intruder of an exclusive men's club, another underdog like us. In 1970, less than a quarter of American journalists were women. Female sports-writers were even rarer. They faced discrimination, harassment, and intimidation, not only from their male colleagues, but also from coaches and players.

Women did not gain access to postgame locker room interviews until a federal court decision in 1978. Subsequently, Mary Garber was more than once hauled from locker rooms by coaches affronted by her presence. Yet there she would be the next day, unflinching, ready with thoughtful questions that made us feel acknowledged and appreciated.

A dedicated reporter, she broke barriers, not by putting her head down and steamrolling her way into newsrooms, but by persistence, a talent for accuracy and clarity, and a way of disarming everyone she interviewed.

Mary Garber's mettle had been tested while covering extremely sensitive topics in the Deep South. Prominent among them was racial discrimination at a time when such things were not apt to win favor with powerbrokers. Confident, unshrinking, and rigidly professional, Garber had a way of talking to players that made her seem like our favorite aunt. Except that, unlike most aunts, she knew her football inside and out. She also empathized with underdogs, which is why we loved her.

There was one significant difference, however, in our common ground as underdogs. Under Cal Stoll's mentorship, we reached the top of our field in two years. It took Mary Garber considerably longer. And while we lived and breathed football exclusively, she wrote with equal facility about baseball, tennis, track, golf, wrestling, and basketball.

In a career spanning more than six decades, Mary Garber garnered more than forty awards, including induction into the U.S. Basketball Writers Hall of Fame in 2002. Notably, in 2005, she became the first woman to receive the prestigious Red Smith Award, given by the Associated Press Sports Editors to a writer or editor who has made major contributions to sports journalism. The fact she was so honored despite having written for the relatively local *Winston-Salem Journal* speaks volumes about her prowess with a pen. Other Red Smith honorees include the likes of Mitch Albom, Frank Deford, Rick Reilly, Dave Anderson, Dick Schaap, Bob Ryan, Bud Collins, and Dave Kindred, whose ink has graced such renowned national publications as the *New York Times, Washington Post, Boston Globe,* and *Sports Illustrated.*

I doubt anyone on the team knew of her past or her accolades, among them, a 1967 plaque from Winston-Salem Tennis for her "keen interest in sports." Acknowledgments of greatness are not always accompanied by national acclaim, but I'm sure Mary Garber took it in stride as she always did, and was genuinely grateful for the pen that came with the plaque, inscribed, "Your warm personal charm, tact, integrity, patience, tolerance, and good humor combined with your writing ability have earned you this tribute."

Physically, Mary Garber was easy to miss. She was barely five feet tall and I doubt she weighed more than a hundred pounds. And she was always calm. If she was gunning for a deadline, players speaking to her as she scribbled notes could not tell. Likewise, if she was disinterested in the topic, she didn't show it.

She made everyone she spoke with—including twenty-year-old football players away from home for the first time—feel important, as if she had been waiting years for the wisdom we imparted. She had a talent for making the mundane interesting. Her print version of every game she covered, every long practice she sat in the hot sun watching, every Cal Stoll pep talk to the Sportsmen's Club, displayed as much enthusiasm as if she'd just returned from a walk on the moon and couldn't wait to tell you about it.

As a young girl, Garber had witnessed Wake Forest's ups and downs firsthand. Though born in New York City, she was a townie to the core, having moved to

Winston-Salem at age eight in 1924, the year the Demon Deacon football team went 7-2 under Hank Garrity.

After graduating from Hollins College (now University), an all-women's college in Roanoke, Virginia, she began a journalistic career that eventually led her to us. In 1944, when the high school sports reporter at the *Twin City Sentinel* in Winston-Salem left to serve in the U.S. Navy, Garber began covering sports and never looked back. She transitioned to full-time in 1946, the only woman covering sports in the region, and one of only a handful in the entire country.

In an oral history interview for the Washington Press Club, Garber recalls how no one looked askance at a female reporter on the sidelines, "The high school kids and the coaches were so delighted that *somebody* was coming around to cover them, that I think I could have been a two-headed monkey and they wouldn't have cared."

A truly colorblind journalist, she remained unaffected by Southern politics concerning race. At a time when segregation was the rule of the land, she covered sports for two Black high schools and Winston-Salem State University, a Black institution, and became a strong advocate for Black athletes and coaches. "I think sports was probably the first place to break down and bring in Black news because sports people are just way ahead of everybody, anyhow," Garber says in the oral history.

Garber's death at age 92 in 2008 merited an obituary in the *New York Times*. The piece quotes her in an interview she had with National Public Radio in 2000. "When I first started, in the '40s, I went to one of the local colleges, and I had press credentials, and they wouldn't let me sit in the press box because women were not allowed to sit in the press box," Garber said. "And while I was talking with the sports information director, there was a little boy hopping up and down in the aisles in the press box, and he could sit there, but I couldn't."

After that incident, she added a note to her press tag that read, "Women and children are not allowed in the press box," implying that only *males*, regardless of age, were granted entry.

Only once was I honored to be the target of Mary Garber's illustrious pen. The story was about me becoming a starter, a piece a normal beat reporter would have churned out in a paragraph or two. But Garber was not a normal beat reporter. I had been promoted to first string, and she knew how hard I had worked to get there.

A master of nuance, Garber was adept at drawing readers into an article. Rather than "DODA TO START," she dug in a bit. She picked out details, turning a simple on-field promotion into something worth reading. The result was four columns in the *Journal* with a photo of me making a catch. The headline and deck ran, "HARD WORK BRINGS SUCCESS, Dave Doda Becomes Valuable Deacon."

She didn't turn the spotlight on me because she thought I was special; she put in that extra effort for every player on the team. Then she went further. She mentioned a new name I had acquired from Cal Stoll.

Most reporters on a Sunday night after a game could be found at home, relaxing, but Mary often attended our postgame reviews to see what she might learn. As the coaches went over the game film following our loss to Virginia, she caught Stoll's comment about some of my missed blocking assignments.

"Doda, for an atomic physicist, you sure blew a lot of assignments." After this, I became known in some circles as "The Mad Scientist." The nickname was pure Cal Stoll.

Acquiring a moniker, complimentary or otherwise, is a mark of distinction among athletes. Garber included Coach's comment in an article. Having her share with the readers of the *Winston-Salem Journal* that I was so honored was, frankly, thrilling.

Mary Garber penned feature stories on every player, giving special attention not only to standouts but to fringe players, assuring each would have his own fifteen minutes of fame. For many of us, those pint-sized doses of recognition in her columns represented the pinnacle of our athletic celebrity, preserved forever in newspaper clippings sent home to proud parents.

THE DRAFT

When I was a student at Wake Forest, disparate views concerning U.S. involvement in Vietnam split the country into two equally zealous camps. On one side was Vice President Spiro Agnew's "Silent Majority," a group whose mantra "My Country, Right or Wrong" left no room for debate. On the other, a growing group who saw the lengthening war as costly, unwinnable, and without purpose.

A period of intense social and political upheaval, the late 1960s was not an easy landscape for young people to navigate. However, during football season and the long months leading up to it, life on the outside, no matter how chaotic, amounted to little more than background noise. Preparing hard and playing to the best of our abilities were the only things that mattered.

With one unavoidable exception. An event so life-changing, the most focused among us could not block it out of his consciousness: The Vietnam War Selective Service Lottery, commonly called "The Draft." In Washington, D.C., the Selective Service System announced its first draft since 1942. The war in Vietnam was escalating. More troops were needed, and my generation was the supply chain.

For a few hours on the night of December 1, 1969, time stood still. Our entire team was a jumble of nerves. With our college deferments gone, the deciding order in which young men were drafted was now completely random. At Wake Forest, players never talked about it, but the prospect of being chosen early hung over each of our heads like lightning waiting to strike.

The entire process was televised live, the cameras aimed at a small stage in a nondescript Selective Service building office. Men in gray suits stood around a glass cylinder, only slightly larger than an office wastebasket. Visible through the container's transparent exterior were 366 brown capsules, each concealing a slip of paper with a date on it. Congressman Alexander Pirnie (R-NY), a member of the House Armed Services Committee, reached in with his hand and drew out the first capsule.

As each capsule was opened, the date it contained was placed on a tote board in the order picked next to the numbers 001 through 366. For such a bland exercise, the numbers held inescapable consequences. Those whose birthdates were placed next to the lowest numbers would be the first ones drafted.

After our loss to Miami ended our 1969 season on a sour note, Cal Stoll never mentioned the upcoming draft in any postseason communications. I know he was paying attention, though. Unlike a game, the lottery results were not something he or his coaching staff could prepare for or defend against. There was no special play to call, no halftime adjustment to counter an opponent's strategy, and no substitutions. Worst of all, there was no way to chart a path forward based on how many players he might lose. There was also no way of knowing who among the 18-year-old recruits the assistant coaches were traveling to meet would, come August, be heading for boot camp instead of summer practice.

The coaches' vision for our team—our objectives for the next two years— could be easily upended by the draft. Our upcoming season came down to chance, never mind classes, graduation, and life after Wake Forest.

Among the players, the topic of Vietnam and the draft was rarely, if ever, discussed. If we had opinions about the war and our potential role in it, we kept such thoughts to ourselves. Even today, I have no idea what my teammates were thinking as the numbers were drawn. For the few hours it took to complete the lottery, though, I imagine that making blocks and scoring touchdowns wasn't on anyone's to-do list.

We were all subject to the needs of our local draft boards. I had registered in Hackensack, New Jersey, and I knew the odds. Across the country, the rule of thumb was that the first third of the birthdays would be drafted, the second third might be drafted, and the final third would be safe.

The drawing began at 8 p.m. For those listening to radio broadcasts, including me, the process was psychological torture. One by one the dates were drawn: September 14. April 24. December 30. On campuses across the country, the event prompted circus-like parties, with winners and losers alike drinking heavily.

To calm my nerves, I drove to the Winston-Salem Memorial Coliseum to watch Wake Forest's basketball team's opener against Ohio State. Four of the five starters were guys in my class: Charlie Davis, Gil McGregor, Neil Pastushok, and Bob (Posey) Rhoads. We didn't sit in the student cheering section; instead, as was our custom, we sat together at one end with the other members of the football team, all wearing our black and gold varsity jackets. It was an exciting game, though we lost 96-92.

Afterward, three friends and I drove the two miles back from the Coliseum and parked in the dorm parking lot, listening to the results being called on the local station WTOB. Between stretches of music and commercials, the DJs announced one hundred dates at a time in the order drawn. By the time we tuned in, one through one hundred had already been announced. As there was no way of knowing if my birthday was among them, I held tightly to the hope that it wasn't.

As the second one hundred were drawn, I prayed my birthday wouldn't be among them. When it wasn't, I became somewhat relieved but at the same time even more nerve-wracked because now there was an almost 40 percent chance my birthdate had been picked in the first one hundred.

The long interludes of music and commercials were excruciating because they only delayed the inevitable. We sat in the car, in the darkness of the parking lot. Waiting. Capsules two hundred to three hundred were drawn, and still my birthday was not announced. Now I was really panicking, because it meant one of two things: I was either completely safe or totally screwed.

Finally, June 9th was announced, the 335th capsule drawn. The long wait was over. I breathed a grateful sigh of relief, safe in the knowledge I could continue my education and stay at Wake Forest. Blind destiny had mercifully allowed me to continue wearing the shiny gold and black helmet of the Demon Deacons—not the drab olive, steel pot helmet of an American G.I.

Miraculously, not one of my teammates ended up being drafted. But there were repercussions for many others. The next day, all over campus, handwritten signs popped up on curbsides or hung out of dorm windows announcing news such as "#5 - Going to Canada."

In the ensuing months, long lines of cars carrying an estimated 50,000 to 90,000 draftable young men headed to Canada. Some stayed in the provinces, eventually becoming Canadian citizens, while most returned to the U.S. after President Jimmy Carter, one day into his presidency in 1977, granted all draft evaders an unconditional pardon, as he had promised during his campaign.

In Winston-Salem, the American Friends Service Committee opened an office for draft counseling. Nine of the fifteen counselors were Wake Forest students. Its primary purpose, said its chairman, was advisory. "We are not trying to convince anyone to avoid the draft. We want only to explain the options available."

By April, when spring practices began, there was no further mention of the draft, at least among my teammates and me. We had other things to do. I, for one, was grateful I'd be able to do them.

STARTING OVER: 1970

No one would have faulted Cal Stoll for lying low and letting the dust settle after a 3-7 season that included more than one shellacking. But for myself and the others who had lived under his tutelage for the better part of a year, what he did came as no surprise. Coach was not going to sit around lamenting our less-than-stellar record; he forged ahead at full speed.

Just two weeks after our lopsided, season-ending loss to Miami, Stoll spoke at the Reynolds High School football banquet. He told his audience at the Elks Club in Winston-Salem to "dream a dream, then do something about it yourself. Set your sights on a goal that you think you cannot reach, then go for it." The man was an indefatigable optimist, bringing the same conviction to a high school sports team banquet as he did to our postgame speeches, win or lose.

It was impossible not to absorb Stoll's glass-half-full spirit. By December, we found ourselves at the high point of the wondrous arc that comes with playing a sport that starts anew each year. The past is locked away, if not utterly forgotten, and the future is always bright.

With a coach like Cal Stoll, there was no time to feel sorry for ourselves or hang on to anger over what had been a largely disappointing season. That anger, along with the tears running down our cheeks in the Miami locker room, had long dried up by the first of January.

For most of us, there was next year. For those seniors whose football careers came to a close in the Hurricanes' visiting locker room, they at least had their memories, bittersweet though they were.

We developed a sort of amnesia, a blissful forgetting that allowed us to plan how we'd make amends for our dismal season. It was a dream based on Stoll's stubborn refusal to acknowledge the critics, and his abiding confidence we would turn things around.

For converts of Coach Cal's unflagging optimism, which included twenty-one returning lettermen—plus others like me still fighting for a spot in the starting lineup—it was a short but exquisite time when all things seemed possible. But back in the real world, below the surface of Stoll's Pollyannish perspective, we harbored well-guarded doubts about how each of us would fit into his master plan.

Of course, there had been slivers of excellence in our losses, too small to make a difference, and brief exhilaration at our few wins. But those feelings were fleeting. Embedded within each pounding we took, however, lay a lesson we could use later. What remained to be seen was whether or not we had enough players willing to learn from those poundings.

Stoll and his coaches didn't even bother to unpack after the Miami game. They came home, briefly reunited with their families, and headed out on the recruiting trail the very next day. By February 1970, they had signed 32 players from 17 states, though that impressive number was contingent on the players meeting Wake Forest and the ACC's stringent academic standards, rejecting other offers, and making the arrangement formal by signing a national letter of intent on May 6.

Stoll told veteran sports reporter Mary Garber that he and his staff had recruited for balance and size, faster backs and bigger linemen. Two of the linemen he hoped to bring in weighed over 250 pounds, he said. Even in the depths of rebuilding, Stoll held tight to his sense of humor. "We are tired of being small and slow," he quipped. "Now, we will be big and slow."

None of us worried much about Stoll's recruiting efforts. Big and slow or not, NCAA regulations prevented incoming freshmen from playing varsity, a rule that would not change until 1972. We might use the incoming freshmen as occasional fodder on the practice field after Stoll's drills had thinned our ranks, but no high school kid coming to Wake Forest in August of 1970 would affect our immediate goals. None of those hopefuls had the slightest idea what lay in store for them, and I can guarantee no coach on the recruiting trail told them about winter conditioning drills or protracted spring practices that left even the toughest players puking on the sidelines.

Veterans of the 1969 season who had not graduated formed the nucleus of the 1970 team. As we ran endless wind sprints in Reynolds Gymnasium, we had three concerns. First, those of us who were only bit actors during the 1969 season—watching games from the sidelines—desperately wanted to start. Second, those who had been starters wished to remain so and would do whatever it took to ensure as much. Third, we were fed up with the constant chirping from critics about our ineptness. And this was before the preseason articles with their cruel analyses began to appear in the magazines. Even as we started our second round of winter drill sessions under Stoll, we braced our psyches for the inevitable onslaught of criticism from the media. The same sad refrain: We were small and slow and would never match up against stronger teams.

By then, however, we had a solution: We stopped paying attention.

In January 1970, we were ready for the internal competition and the coaching staff's continuous evaluations and tests. Coach's winter conditioning program would not be a surprise, nor would his four-hour spring practices. We'd been through that already and emerged stronger.

We were teammates, sharing meals and classes, but whatever friendships we had would be temporarily set aside while we strived to reach our individual and team goals. At this point we knew one another's strengths and weaknesses—who could be counted on in the fourth quarter, whose lungs would give out first, and whose spirit would never break. Each player would do whatever he could to draw attention to himself and earn a starting position.

There was one slight problem. We hadn't counted on the addition of six junior college transfers: four running backs, a quarterback, and one defensive end, all of them eligible to play immediately.

One of those junior college transfers was Larry Hopkins, a 5-foot, 10-inch, 205-pound running back with power and speed. He had been recruited from Lees McRae Junior College in the mountain town of Banner Elk, North

Carolina. Stoll showed his intuitive understanding of team dynamics when he assigned our best returning running back in 1969, junior Steve Bowden, to show the recruit around campus and talk up the football program.

It would prove an auspicious meeting, though surely an awkward one, as Bowden pointed out campus landmarks to the man who might take his job. In due time, "Hoppy," as we nicknamed him, would show the coaches he was equally at ease running around players or powering over the top of them.

As the year began, each of us had his own challenges. Even those who knew they would start would have to be in tip-top shape and remain injury-free, a tall order given the physical demands Stoll placed on us.

Some players' positions were solid. Others, including me, would have to fight for every minute of playing time. As winter training began, our minds were not thinking about who we'd be playing in the fall, but rather, if we'd be starting or sitting on the bench watching others live out our dreams.

Preseason All-America contender Win Headley, along with Terry Kuharchek, Dick Chulada, Dick Bozoian, and Ed Bradley, had established themselves as the team's defensive leaders. They would start. Gary German, one of the biggest guys on the team at 6 feet, 3 inches, and 215 pounds, would join them midseason following starting center Nick Vrhovac's emergency appendectomy. There was no question about that core group's talents or their positions.

But Stoll threw a few curve balls into the mix, challenging players to demonstrate their versatility. Part of assembling the puzzle required him to move some players out of positions they were used to and assign them new ones. Stoll was considering moving Gary Johnson, one of ten high school quarterbacks recruited for the previous fall's freshmen team, to tailback. Stoll already had more QBs than he needed, and Gary had already shown his ability to adapt, having previously switched to wide receiver and safety on the freshmen squad. "After they saw me throw a football," Gary recalls, "We all knew I would never play that position at Wake." My freshman roommate, Terry Kuharchek, was also recruited as a quarterback but switched to defensive back sophomore year. He worked hard to stay there, earning accolades as an All-ACC three-year starter.

Terry, Gary, and the other freshmen QB recruits all lost their signal-calling roles to left-handed Larry "Russ" Russell, who had earned his spot in the starting lineup with his darting runs, toughness, and ability to shake off mistakes. But despite being the hardest working and fittest guy on the team, even he was not a shoo-in for first-string quarterback in 1970. At 5 feet, 11 inches, Russ had taken far too many hits in 1969, and his size and passing consistency were both suspect in Stoll's view. He and drop-back passer Jim McMahen, who had led the freshman squad at QB the previous fall, were forced to compete against each other all spring to prove who belonged in the starting lineup.

There were questions everywhere, not the least of which was what offense Stoll would decide to run to counter our traditional problem of being, as so many said, "too small and too slow" to challenge our Division I opponents.

Steve Bowden, a strong inside runner during the 1969 season, had heard Stoll's critique that he lacked outside speed. Hopkins and James W. "Junior" Moore, another junior college transferee, both had the speed Stoll was looking for, but no one was sure how the backfield would operate once the hitting started in earnest.

Gary Winrow had a lock on tight end. He led the team in receptions in 1969 and had a talent for adding yards afterward, his robust frame breaking tackles that would have stopped smaller men. Against Clemson in 1969, he set a season single-game receiving record with nine catches.

Our linemen, both offensive and defensive, were immune to the "too small" descriptor assigned to them. Bill Bobbora, Vince Nedimyer, and Nick Vrhovac spent the offseason preparing to toss the criticism aside. Ed Stetz, a linebacker of moderate stature, had made a point in 1969 that size has no bearing on aggressiveness. He was ready to prove his point once again.

Our returning defensive backs, including Dick Bozoian, Terry Kuharchek, and Pat McHenry, had been sorely tested in 1969. They were girding themselves to do it all over again.

And so it went, each man striving to carve out a place within Stoll's grand scheme, thus ensuring our entry into the annals of Wake Forest football.

In February, the athletic department tossed us yet another challenge. Its director, Gene Hooks, announced that Wake Forest had added an eleventh game to its 1970 season, this one against national power Nebraska. We were scheduled to play them in Lincoln on September 12 in front of 68,000 screaming Nebraska fans. It was just one more thing to think about, as if we didn't have enough on our plates.

While we ended our 1969 season being routed by Miami, Nebraska demolished Georgia 45-6 in the Sun Bowl, making headlines nationwide. But holding fast to Stoll's steadfast optimism, we added the Cornhuskers to our list of motivators, viewing them as another opportunity to prove wrong everyone who had written us off.

As winter conditioning continued, we felt something building within our team—unity born out of suffering, fortitude strengthened by disappointment, and a hunger we hoped would transform us from perennial underdogs into conference contenders.

A SEASON OF
CIVIL UNREST

On a campus that had, at least on paper, ended segregation in 1962, Wake Forest's antiquated attitudes regarding racial inequality remained deeply rooted. In the late 1960s, despite the growing numbers of students and professors whose leanings could be considered progressive, there were many more who clung unabashedly to the past.

Caught between the fading echoes of one era and the uncertain birth pains of another, Wake Forest was a latecomer to the Civil Rights movement. Throughout the decade of the sixties and beyond, the university continued almost exclusively to attract White students from wealthy Southern families, a practice that created a less than harmonious social climate for our Black teammates. For them, the Jim Crow era wasn't some vestige of the past, it was life writ large.

No one had to look very far to see overt racism being played out in real time. In October 1967, James Eller was killed by police on the front steps of his home in Winston-Salem while resisting arrest for public drunkenness. The police withheld details of the incident for over a week, and in November, a judge dismissed murder charges. Four days of rock hurling, looting, and arson ensued as rioters defied a 1,200-man armed guard in what was called the worst outbreak of racial violence in North Carolina in the 20th century.

I witnessed fallout from this historic episode firsthand. That November, after spending Thanksgiving break back home in New Jersey, I rode in a taxi from the Greensboro airport back to campus. As the cabbie drove along Interstate 40, I saw National Guard tanks blocking every exit and entrance leading into or out of the city of Winston-Salem while the riots raged. It was a deeply unsettling sign of the times.

By 1967 the Civil Rights movement had spilled over into the arena of college football. At the University of California, Berkeley, thirty-five Black football players boycotted spring practice until more Black coaches were hired.

In spring 1968, when Stoll was in his last year as an assistant coach at Michigan State University, twenty-four MSU players walked out of practice, vowing not to return until their demands for more Black coaches, trainers, and cheerleaders were met.

Fourteen Black players were suspended from the football team at the University of Wyoming for wearing black armbands to a meeting with the school's athletic director to discuss alleged acts of racial discrimination by Brigham Young University, their opponent that week. BYU was affiliated with the Mormon Church, which denied leadership positions to people of African descent, claiming that their dark skin was "the mark of the curse of Ham." They filed a $1.1 million lawsuit against the university.

At Syracuse University in 1969, Black football players advocated for an end to discrimination along with other reforms that would benefit all student-athletes. Nine Black players, erroneously dubbed the "Syracuse 8" by the media, eventually boycotted spring practice and then the 1969 season because their head coach, Ben Schwartzwalder, reneged on his promise to hire a Black assistant. The school president ordered Schwartzwalder to hire one Black coach, which he eventually did, but he also kicked the boycotting players off the team. By the 1970 season, Syracuse had a Black coach and no Black players.

Wake Forest was the first all-White school in the South to be integrated. Stoll's predecessor, Bill Tate, brought the first two Black athletes—defensive lineman Bob Grant and wide receiver Butch Henry—to the school in 1964, at a time when North Carolina and Winston-Salem still held tightly to segregation.

His decision was not without consequences—he received threatening letters from members of the Ku Klux Klan.

Still, Tate remained committed. He spoke candidly with his Black recruits about the adversity they might encounter, particularly during road games in the Deep South. Together, they made history. That 1964 season, Grant and Henry helped lead the Demon Deacons to a 5–5 record, and Tate was named ACC Coach of the Year.

In the spring of 1970, there were eight Black players on our 1970 Wake Forest team out of a total of seventy-six. One of them was the aforementioned Larry Hopkins. Blessed with a combination of speed and power, he brought far more than athleticism to our campus. A dean's list chemistry major, he had based his decision to attend Wake as much on academic opportunity as on football.

Having grown up in Panama City, a stone's throw from the Alabama border on the Florida Panhandle, Larry had no illusions about what he was stepping into at Wake Forest. Neither did Junior Moore, Gary Terrell, cousins Joel and Steve Bowden, Ken Garrett, Mike Howlette, and Archie Logan—our other Black teammates. These weren't just athletes; they were resilient, unperturbed, ambitious young men. They understood the less-than-ideal social environment that awaited a Black student on an overwhelmingly White campus in the Deep South. But they were willing to deal with it because of the benefits a Wake Forest degree would grant them. Plus, they could play football in the Atlantic Coast Conference, where they might attract the attention of NFL scouts. Either way, their future would be bright.

Larry Hopkins became a vital part of Stoll's new offense in 1970. But his impact extended far beyond the playing field. After graduating with honors, he turned down an offer from the New England Patriots, choosing instead to attend Bowman School of Medicine, now the Wake Forest School of Medicine. After completing his residency in obstetrics and gynecology at the Medical College of Virginia, he enlisted in the United States Air Force, where his assignment led him to Shreveport, Louisiana. He rose to the rank of major.

Steve Bowden and Archie Logan went on to become clergymen. I don't think that's a coincidence. Stoll and his assistants possessed a talent for recruiting players with inner strength, faith in what Wake Forest offered, and an innate ability to maintain equilibrium despite the civil unrest of the time. They deliberately sought out players who could shrug off the inevitable criticism that came with being a member of the Wake Forest football team. Black players, in particular, needed that fortitude. When recruiting our Black 1970 teammates, I have no doubt Stoll told them precisely what lay in store and promised they would be safe under his watch.

As a Floridian growing up in the '50s and '60s, Hopkins was all too familiar with the Jim Crow South, which in North Carolina in 1970 had only just begun to fade. For Blacks, it meant segregated schools, restrooms, water fountains, restaurants, pools, churches, golf courses, and beaches, to name a few.

To players like me who grew up in the Northeast, racial segregation was an unfamiliar concept, a strange and archaic holdover from a Civil War that had ended more than a hundred years before. Experiencing the South for the first time, I could still spot the legacy of these laws, signs of which were very much present in 1970. Naively, I viewed them as an odd curiosity that I believed was now part of the past. I was wrong, of course.

Hopkins experienced overt discrimination in the fall of 1970 following the completion of a chemistry test. The professor who had administered the test challenged Larry's level of intelligence and questioned his integrity, telling him no Black football player could have possibly solved one of the equations—the implication being that he must have cheated. Apparently, the professor either did not know or did not care that Larry had been a pre-engineering major before transferring to Wake Forest from Lees McCrae. Callously, and without just cause, the professor refused to give him credit for his correct answer.

Beth Norbery Hopkins, Larry's widow, remembers how her then-boyfriend collapsed in tears afterward, questioning his ability to continue pursuing a degree in chemistry while maintaining the high standards he'd set for himself. The couple sent a telegram to Larry's father, then posted to Germany with the U.S. Air Force, telling him what had transpired. The elder Hopkins immediately sent his own telegram to Wake Forest's president, Ralph Scales, calling attention to the injustice.

Although the professor never changed the test grade, he was officially put on notice that President Scales would not tolerate unfair grading practices and racial discrimination. In the end, Larry earned a B in the course, a small victory in a much larger struggle.

The trajectory of Hopkins' life after Wake Forest reveals what an amazing person he was. He later returned to Winston-Salem and helped establish the

Women's Health Center, which specialized in improving prenatal care and reducing infant mortality while raising the level of healthcare for African American women in the area. In 1986, he began serving on Wake Forest University's Board of Trustees, and in 1996 became an assistant professor of Obstetrics and Gynecology at his alma mater, while heading up the department.

Ten years after the chemistry test incident, Larry was on campus for a Trustees meeting. As fate would have it, he ran into the professor who so shamelessly discriminated against him. Without rancor, Larry calmly told him, "I am on the Board of Trustees, so I am *your* boss now. You tried to discourage me, but here I am."

As for the football team, Coach Stoll was adamant that racism would not be tolerated. We were an underdog team who, more than any single thing, needed to support one another *unconditionally* if we were to rid ourselves of our losing persona. It was tacitly understood that no player, regardless of race, was to engage in any action or speech, overtly or otherwise, that might be interpreted as offensive. This understanding, bolstered by our shared desire to play and keep our scholarships, created, at least outwardly, a team free of racial tensions.

On the field, we were colorblind. We all got along, united by our goal to prove ourselves capable of competing at the highest level. Black or White, Southerners or not, there were no tensions over racial issues within our ranks. Like any random group of people, we came from different backgrounds, held different philosophies, and maintained different beliefs. We weren't necessarily all best friends, but we had each other's backs and shared one overarching vision: play Division I football and graduate from a top school.

Despite these bonds, one notable difference stood out: The path of our Black teammates was rife with stress-inducing obstacles White players could scarcely imagine. If White players felt tested by Stoll's drills and hellish practices, they had only to retreat to their dorm rooms and classes, where they blended smoothly into everyday campus life. For our Black teammates, the trials didn't end when they stepped off the practice field. They continued in classrooms, dormitories, and at social events—virtually every corner of the Wake Forest campus. One of the most onerous of these was the tradition of blasting "Dixie"—a racist tribute to the Confederate cause and its defense of slavery—out the windows of every Southern frat house prior to home football games.

Beth Hopkins (then Norbrey) recalls what it was like to be a Black student during those years. "When I arrived, there were fewer than 20 Black students on campus. We survived by remaining true to our ethnicity." She also recalls the remarkable lives of her peers despite the hurdles they had to overcome due to their skin color. "The Black athletes of my generation graduated from Wake Forest and pursued careers in law, investment banking, medicine, divinity, and education. Together, we taught Wake Forest students that successful academic achievements were cross-cultural."

It was not an easy lesson to convey, especially when prejudice came not just from fellow students but from authority figures. "There were battles to fight on all fronts," Beth remembers. "Fraternities were not our worst enemies. There were professors who vocalized their displeasure about the presence of Black students on campus because they felt that genetically they could not compete."

Institutional racism manifested in unexpected ways. When Beth was voted Wake Forest Homecoming Queen, the first Black woman ever accorded the honor, the school newspaper chose not to cover the event, ignoring the milestone completely. The college's yearbook did note it, but with a cruel twist. Known as *The Howler*, the yearbook featured a photo of Beth wearing her Homecoming Queen crown, but the image had been altered to give her two black eyes. "I am sure the [yearbook] staff was amused, but my family and I were not," she said.

Despite the adversities faced by our Black teammates, Stoll held us together as a team. He did this not by decrying racial disharmony at team meetings or offering sympathy—he believed sympathy encouraged weakness, and weakness was unacceptable in his eyes—but by shutting it out entirely. In his mind, we weren't Black or White football players, but a single team on a mission that left no room for petty divisions.

Meanwhile, outside our relatively serene campus, North Carolina told a different story. In Burlington in May 1969, a year before the Kent State shootings, riots broke out at the recently integrated Walter Williams High School after a Black girl was denied a spot on the cheerleading team. The protest soon grew to include students at nearby Jordan-Sellers High School and local colleges. A fight between White and Black students and the governor's subsequent declaration of a state of emergency prompted the calling in of the National Guard, and by the end of the second day of protesting, many stores were on fire, and an unarmed fifteen-year-old Black boy lay dead, riddled by police gunfire.

Later that month, National Guardsmen and demonstrators faced off again in a five-day confrontation that became known as the Greensboro Uprising. Protests broke out at the all-Black James B. Dudley High School after school officials refused to recognize the validity of a write-in candidate for student council—despite election results being overwhelmingly in his favor—allegedly because of his activism in the Black Power movement.

Students at nearby North Carolina Agricultural & Technical State University got involved, with police and students exchanging gunfire. After A&T student Willie Grimes was killed by gunshot from a passing car while walking a group of friends to a restaurant, the violence escalated exponentially. The subsequent invasion of the A&T campus by 600 National Guardsmen, complete with tanks and a helicopter, was described at the time as "the most massive armed assault ever made against an American university."

Our coach made no mention of these incidents while we practiced. We ran drills, we tackled, we memorized plays. The world outside did not exist within his framework. There were battles to fight on every front in the real world, but in his mind, he was preparing us for only one: to prevail on the gridiron. Viewed through the lens of half-century of history, Stoll's blinders-on philosophy seems harsh today—even dismissive—of the real struggles our Black teammates faced. But it served its purpose.

Assistant coach Oval Jaynes, a man with deep Southern roots, captured the atmosphere of our team with a story that reveals his no-nonsense approach: "When I was in college at Appalachian, Black students were a rarity. There weren't many at school or on the team," he recalled. "The first Black athlete that I coached was at Wake Forest University in 1969. Early on, I pulled him aside, looked him in the eye, and told him, 'You are Black, and I am White. If that is a problem, you need to let me know now. The only yardstick that I will use to measure you is how you block and tackle.'"

All of us, Jaynes, Stoll and his assistants, and Black and White players alike, had been thrown into the eddies of a shameful history no one could change. We were idealistic kids, unbowed by the weight of the past and innocently hopeful about the future. United by a common purpose, we got along without incident in the locker room and on the field. The rest of the imperfect world, we believed, would soon follow.

THE
PUZZLE

A s 1970 dawned, Cal Stoll had in front of him, unassembled, a 77-piece virtual jigsaw puzzle. The puzzle pieces, nineteen returning lettermen plus thirty rising sophomores, lay scattered across his mental workbench.

Over the next several months, Stoll and his assistants would conduct a grand experiment. Except for a few shoo-ins whose positions were all but guaranteed, we would be tested, studied, and evaluated before being accepted or rejected. By the end of the summer, we'd either be starters or occasional contributors from the bench.

No one wanted to watch the 1970 season from the sidelines. Starters from 1969 could not rest on whatever laurels they had earned the previous year. All but a handful would have to prove themselves still worthy, earning their positions by beating out teammates eager to replace them.

Once Stoll found the right combination, he then needed to figure out how best to use it. It was a daunting assignment. How could he transform a 3-7 team many felt was incapable of competing in Division I into a winner? The pieces that lay scattered in front of him would have to fit perfectly. And, once completed, they would have to stay together, remain healthy, and move into the season with a purpose. There was no sense in forcing an ill-fitting piece into an opening that, at first glance, seemed reasonable. One wrong choice could weaken the entire structure. Everything had to mesh seamlessly.

Stoll knew he could control only so many things. Questions abounded. As we began our winter workouts, he tried to influence our attitudes while running us ragged. He told us repeatedly that we were to play every down as if it were the last. He reminded us that in a four-quarter game, three or four plays can decide the outcome.

After Nebraska was added to the schedule, our critics, never short of something to say, agreed on two things. We would be better than 1969, but with our lack of depth we would be lucky to emerge with the same 3-7 record. Told that, Stoll stoically replied, "We're not going to lie down and play dead for anyone." He had recently announced the signing of thirty-one incoming freshmen and six junior college transfers for the 1970 season. The pressure on us to compete for starting positions only intensified with the knowledge that reinforcements were on their way. Incoming talent might replace us if we didn't measure up.

There would be keen competition for quarterback. The elusive, left-handed scrambler Larry Russell, who had shown flashes of brilliance both running and passing, would be challenged by Jim Ryan and drop-back passer Jim McMahen, who could throw the long ball. All three would be tossed into the mix, their strengths and weaknesses weighed and measured during each practice.

I was one of the scattered pieces in Stoll's puzzle box. Despite being the only returning defensive end from the previous fall, the defensive coordinator used me in practices as a blocking dummy or a ball carrier, to be battered by others fighting for a starting position at outside linebacker or defensive end. I wasn't the most talented player on the team; but even so, other players came up to me and asked, "Dodes, what's going on?"

Languishing on defense, I had not yet shown I could be a tight end. I knew I could. I had one glimmer of hope: My linebacker coach hated my guts. He thought I was a worthless hippie because of my colorful, fringed scarf. He would be thrilled to have me out from under his jurisdiction.

Figuring I had nothing to lose, I walked into Stoll's office and asked him to switch me to tight end. At the time our offense featured a split end, a tight end, and a flanker—a standard pro-style offense. My good friend and classmate, Gary Winrow, was already starting at tight end, so basically, I was requesting to be his backup.

Sometime later Stoll told the local press, "David walked into my office and asked to switch to offense as a tight end. He had gone through hell and back just like everybody else and survived. He was getting his degree in physics and would be moving on with his life. I was going to let him play anywhere he wanted to." That spring before the 1970 season, I switched to the offense as the second-string tight end behind my classmate Gary. I was now in my preferred slot; however, I still needed to prove to Coach Stoll that I was truly worthy, because that is how he was.

My opportunity came one hot, windless August practice leading up to the 1970 season, the air so humid you could've cut it with a knife. I was working as a tight end on seven-on-seven drills. With fewer players to contend with, such drills were designed to fine-tune basic moves. It was a good way for Stoll to hone our skills and get the cogs meshing.

Coach called for a "delay over the middle," a play in which the tight end holds for a two-count at the line of scrimmage and then cuts through the open space created when the linebackers rush. In an actual game situation, the defense doesn't know what play is coming. Meanwhile, the safeties, having retreated, are unaware of the tight end's intentions to invade the brief opening for a quick pass.

Theoretically, there would be a gap for me to catch the pass and then cut upfield. It is a high-risk play because the tight end is exposed, an easy target. The play's success hinges on the element of surprise. If it works, there are yards to be gained, in theory anyway. But the theory doesn't pan out when the defense knows what's coming. Cal announced the play in front of all fourteen of us. There would be no surprises.

On the first play from scrimmage, quarterback Larry Russell took the snap. I delayed, then swiftly cut across for his pass. The safety, Frank Fussell, not surprisingly, met me abruptly head-on in the ribs of my outstretched body and pile-drove me into the grass. I held onto the ball.

In a typical practice drill situation, the first-team players would return to the backfield, behind the action, and the second team would run the same drill. This time, however, was different. "Run it again," Stoll barked. We returned to the line of scrimmage. Russell stepped behind center and called for the ball. Same result. My clock was cleaned.

"Run it again," Stoll said.

I continued to line up, catch the pass, and get hammered. I couldn't help thinking about Albert Einstein's definition of insanity: doing the same thing over and over again and expecting different results. By the seventh or eighth time we ran the play, Frank apologized. "Sorry, Dodes," he said.

"Don't worry about it, Frank," I replied. It wasn't his fault. If I wanted to play tight end, I had no choice. And neither did he.

And so it continued. We ran that tight end delay nineteen times without interruption. I only dropped one pass. At some point my whole body became numb. The pain came later that evening when my nerve endings began to reconnect.

After that nineteenth play, Cal Stoll called out, "Next." Then he walked over to me and, in what was a detailed conversation for us, said, "Doda, that was simply a gut check." As it turned out, the fates smiled on me. Stoll eventually moved to a two tight-end offense, creating an opening for me to start.

Our offensive line had gaps, and even Stoll admitted it was too small. He planned to move 6-foot, 220-pound guard Vince Nedimyer to tackle. Departing senior center Joe Dobner had to be replaced, perhaps with Nick Vrhovac, whose only experience at the position was long snapping on punts.

In 1969, we had 6-foot, 4-inch, 245-pound Ed George to open holes at left tackle. Now that he was gone, Stoll would look at another guard, 6-foot, 2-inch, 220-pound Ted Waite, as a replacement, along with Nedimyer, Gerry McGowan, a 6-foot, 5-inch, 245-pound senior, and Bill Bobbora, a 6-foot, 1-inch, 215-pound junior.

Defense was less of a concern. With solid returnees like Win Headley, Ed Bradley, Ed Stetz, Terry Kuharchek, Pat McHenry, and Dick Bozoian, Stoll had at least some pieces in place. Still, there would be other competitions for spots.

Dick Chulada had spent three years waiting to start at defensive tackle. When he arrived as a freshman, he weighed close to 290 pounds. Chulada was working hard to shed the extra weight and show Stoll he was ready, but whether he would or not remained to be seen.

Linebacker Carlyle Pate was returning after a year off. He had dropped out of school after a frustrating, injury-ridden year and was now back and healthy. Two of our defensive players had come to Wake Forest as offensive stars in high school. Terry Kuharchek had arrived as a quarterback but was switched to safety, where he led the team in interceptions in 1969. Stoll needed to know if he'd continue to excel.

Dick Bozoian had been a star running back in high school and arrived at Wake Forest expecting to do the same. He was switched to defense as a cornerback and did well in 1969. Would he be able to keep it up?

It would take Cal Stoll until August before he knew for sure that every position, save one, was assigned to the right athlete. It would be a few games into the season before he found out which offense capitalized on the skills of his quarterbacks.

His first task, though, did not require any tough choices. No matter what offense he eventually decided on, or which player belonged in what position, he could guarantee one thing: We would be physically fit when spring practice began. He also knew that every player who stuck it out that winter and spring—who hung in there regardless, no matter the price—would have the character and resilience to accept whatever changes lay in store. Their commitment and courage would put in place the first and most essential piece of Stoll's puzzle.

NEW YEAR,
NEW MINDSET

The Christmas decorations were packed away, New Year's resolutions still fresh. But looming on the horizon was something we knew all too well. In just one week, we'd be returning to Reynolds Gymnasium for another six-week serving of body-punishing drills from Coach Cal Stoll. While no one who had withstood the brutal 1969 sessions was looking forward to repeating them, something fundamental had changed within us. We wanted to be there.

The veterans on the team had bonded in ways impossible to explain to outsiders. The shared agony we'd experienced in 1969 would not be repeated the same way. Not because the drills would be any easier or we were stronger physically, but because we were fundamentally different.

We had become members of a mutual admiration society, closed to outsiders, even our most loyal supporters. The respect we held for each other could not be quantified. We did not need to articulate it: it was *understood* by each and every one of us.

That unspoken connection was our secret motivation, and it motivated us as we worked out on our own. It sustained us through voluntary predawn runs and solitary weight sessions when no coach was watching. It fed us.

We'd been caught off guard at Stoll's first winter conditioning drills, whose primary goal was to thin the herd by separating those who wanted to wear the uniform from those willing to sacrifice everything for it. We'd ended the season two months before, in tears, having swallowed the bitter pill of a disappointing 3-7 record.

But instead of recoiling at the thought of another disappointing season ahead, that same 3-7 record galvanized us to make a solemn pledge: We would never allow ourselves to live through something like that again.

Cal Stoll's untiring optimism had much to do with our transformation. His belief in us never wavered, even when we doubted ourselves. But our painful memories of 1969—the humiliation, the defeats, the knowledge we could be better—had transformed us from the inside out.

In January 1970, the veterans, eager to prove themselves, looked forward to what lay in store. Newcomers, having been forewarned, had also prepared themselves mentally and physically. We all wanted to be in the best shape of our lives, not because Stoll demanded it, but because we demanded it of ourselves.

Stoll was no longer struggling to identify which players had the grit and desire he was looking for. He had them. The players who showed up at Reynolds that winter had already proven we were in for the ride, however bumpy it would be. We had a demanding fall schedule ahead, an unresolved offensive strategy, and the usual low expectations from our many critics. None of which mattered to us, and Stoll knew that.

We were ready for another round, though our spirits fell the instant we walked into the locker room and spotted six large plastic-lined garbage cans positioned strategically around the room. The year before we had indelicately declared them "the puke buckets"—their very presence a testament to the intensity that awaited us. It was on again.

The 1970 version of Stoll's winter conditioning program sounded very familiar: the squeaking of dozens of athletic shoes against the polished gym floor, the piercing trills of coaches' whistles, the grunts and heavy breathing of teammates pushed to their limits. But this time we were no longer shell-shocked individuals wondering what in God's name Stoll was trying to do to us.

We knew. More importantly, we knew why.

Virtually nothing changed from 1969 except our attitudes. This time around, we had no doubts whatsoever we'd get through it. That was our mindset.

We met every afternoon for an hour straight of sprints, shuttle runs, jumping jacks, push-ups, sit-ups, and down-ups amid the coaches' continuous goading. We shrugged and moved through the drills. No one looked around to see who might quit because we knew no one would. Nor did we look for missing name tags on lockers the next day. We all knew we'd make it. And we did—with one exception, a walk-on junior who clearly had no idea what he'd signed up for.

To keep us on our toes, Stoll added a sinister twist to the finale. The 1969 sessions had each ended with four sets of twenty-five tendon-stretching, arm- and quad-burning down-ups. We'd hit the gym floor, do a push-up, then spring to our feet and run in place until the whistle blew to hit the floor again. After twenty-five, we'd have less than a minute to recover before we did another twenty-five, meaning no one left the gym before making it through 100 down-ups sandwiched between hard running in place.

Stoll called each set of twenty-five a "quarter" to remind us of the need to push ourselves the entire game, to be stronger in the fourth quarter than our opponents. But the 1970 down-ups drill would be slightly different. Stoll had got wind that renowned Notre Dame head coach Ara Parseghian, whose team was predicted to be among the country's best that year, also put his players through four quarters of down-ups at the end of their fitness sessions. So Stoll decided to do Parseghian one better. He tasked us with an additional set, a fifth quarter so to speak, thus establishing ourselves as stronger than even the mighty Fighting Irish.

It didn't matter to us. If Stoll had wanted us to do down-ups until the entire team was prostrate on the floor puking our brains out we would have. That was the difference a year had made. We were no longer mere football players. We were brothers forged in the crucible of Cal Stoll's winter conditioning, ready to take on whatever came next.

TESTING OUR METTLE

Spring practice began on a bright, chilly afternoon in mid-March. It ended as it would for the next six weeks: two-and-a-half hours later, in the dark. Cal Stoll's 1970 puzzle-making project taught us that the road to victory can be fraught with pain. The previous season's 3-7 record hung around our necks like an albatross, and Stoll's strategy included pummeling us into something entirely different. "It looked more like mid-season than opening day," the ever-present Mary Garber wrote in her newspaper column, capturing the intensity that would define our spring. "Tom Harper's defensive line started smacking each other from the start. They were still hitting when the practice ended."

It was no different for the offense I hoped to be a part of. If Stoll was to turn our dismal record around, he needed durable players who could push through the pressure and continue to play. Every aspiring player, including the previous year's starters, was given his own gut check, which was as much about physical endurance as about honing skills.

Coach knew that members of the squad who had played through the trying 1969 season had their heads in the right place. He just wanted to eliminate any doubt that when things got tough we wouldn't break. For that reason, there were no sacred cows, no positions that couldn't be challenged.

As far as we were concerned, we'd made it this far and weren't planning on giving up, no matter what Stoll doled out. There was a silent understanding among the team—an unspoken pact—that we would do whatever was necessary to transform our program. Meanwhile, Coach was testing us in the most literal way possible.

And there were casualties, mostly temporary, but alarming in number. Barely a month into our spring ordeal, injured players filled the sidelines during our annual intra-squad scrimmage, a testament to the savage hitting of the previous four weeks.

Larry Russell, our number one quarterback, watched from the sidelines with an injured shoulder. Jim Pope, who had been shifted from defensive to offensive guard, was out for the rest of the spring with a broken arm. So were running backs Ken Griffith and Randy Ward, offensive guards Tom Colluci and Will Holthouser, and defensive end Al Beard, all sidelined with shoulder, knee, and kidney injuries that would take time to heal.

Ted Waite, another offensive guard, threw out his shoulder during the scrimmage, and no one was sure how long he'd be out. Offensive tackle Gerry McGowan was sidelined with a concussion. Defensive back Gary McCoy and guard Tom Martin, nursing tender hip pointers, joined the other injured spectators. As for anyone not on the Injured Reserve list, including me, we continued to practice, continued to hit, continued to endure.

That spring was unusually chilly for North Carolina, with frequent rain, but Stoll never postponed practice or moved it inside the gym. We practiced outdoors in torrential downpours. The mud sucked at our cleats; drenched jerseys and pads added pounds to our already exhausted frames. Water streamed from our helmets into our eyes as we struggled to see. Still, we hit. Still, we ran. Still, we persevered.

As we jockeyed for starting positions, there were questions to be answered. But Coach Cal was not interested in discussing where we wanted to play and why. We had the skills; he just needed to find the right formula in which to use them.

What he truly cared about was character. Who wanted it more? Who was willing to put it all on the line? Who could be trusted to come through in the clutch? These were the answers Stoll was looking for. He had no intention of building a new team from scratch; he was looking to solidify our common persona. He avowed he would forge a team that embodied the will to win, even if it meant pushing us to our absolute limits to see who would break and who would stand.

There were no warm-ups that spring, no stretches or slow-paced laps around the field to limber up for what was to come during practice. Stoll assumed we were in shape, that when we stepped on the field, we were ready to go. The whistle blew, and immediately we were at full speed, full contact, full intensity.

At the beginning of each practice, we split into our respective groups: ends, running backs, offensive and defensive linemen, defensive backs, and linebackers. For the long afternoon in the fading light, we worked with the assistants to hone specific skills and become comfortable with each other.

At intermittent points during practice, the blast of an air horn cut through the sounds of exertion and instruction. The horn signified that it was one group's turn to be subjected to two new drills while the other groups continued to work on skills. We learned to dread the sound, as it signaled that whatever punishment our bodies were currently enduring was about to intensify.

"Bull in the Ring" was one such drill. And though not unique to Wake Forest, it was particularly severe. It goes like this. When the horn sounds, the selected group moves off to a far corner of the field and forms a circle. One player is directed to the middle of the circle. He is the "bull" surrounded by "matadors."

The assistant coach in charge calls the name of a player in the circle, whose goal is to tackle the bull. The bull spins frantically, trying to identify his attacker so he can brace himself for impact. Sometimes the coach might call two names, causing the bull to be sandwiched between charging teammates. Or he might wait until the bull has staggered to his feet from the previous tackle and then have him hit from behind when he was most vulnerable. Each player in the group had turns as both bull and attacker, thus doubling the chance of injury.

More than fifty years later, I have yet to come up with a good reason for "Bull in the Ring." It teaches no discernible skills, does not improve reflexes—because whatever reflexes we needed were soon numbed—and does not improve fitness, because being continuously blindsided and rammed into the turf for four or five minutes without a break does nothing but cause pain. The NCAA and NFL later banned it due to the high incidence of concussions. Today such drills are rightfully considered reckless and dangerous. For us, they were part of the game.

After everyone in the selected group had been through the rotation, we'd return to our skill drills until it was time for Stoll's second diversion, the "Agilizer." Our personal name for it was "Macrame from Hell."

Off the field, at the far end of the track, Stoll had his assistants string up a rectangular latticework of rope comprising dozens of eighteen-inch squares. The entire grid was suspended twelve inches off the ground. One at a time, players had to navigate at full speed through the grid, pumping their legs and knees high, attempting to enter and exit each square without tripping or becoming entangled in the web. Easier said than done.

When our groups' turn for the Agilizer came, we'd be coming off of drills in which we ran constantly, our legs already rubbery from exertion. In essence, the rope grid was nothing more than a test of coordination when our bodies were least capable of providing it. Very few of us made it through without stopping at some point to regain our balance. Making those high, jumping steps was especially challenging for the larger players on the team.

Each man took his turn and then watched his teammates struggle as he had. Belly-flopping or getting entangled in front of one's teammates added an element of embarrassment to an already frustrating exercise. But those who fell on their faces need not have worried: No one watching gained any pleasure from witnessing their failures. Indeed, if we felt anything at all, it was surely empathy.

There were a great many tests that spring. We continued to do as asked, regardless of how we felt—tired, injured, or uncertain. The transformation Stoll had carefully planned out was beginning to take shape. Players began to assert themselves and claim positions. There was a growing sense within the team that something special was happening. We strengthened our resolve and gained confidence. But Stoll didn't let up. He pushed to the very end, demanding our best even as our bodies willed otherwise.

We never flinched. Not once—despite the pain, the exhaustion, the injuries. Durable athletes, gut-checked and tested for six straight weeks, can do that. Even Stoll noticed. "Things are a lot better than they were this time a year ago," he told Mary Garber at our final practice that spring.

Old Gold & Black sports editor Tom Jennings described the annual intra-squad scrimmage at the conclusion of spring practice. "An aggressive defensive effort and the accurate passing of quarterback Jim McMahen led the Deacons past the favored Demons, 20-0. A crowd of over 2,000 watched the game, the culmination of 20 spring practice sessions with 72 prospective football players. The next time these players don their uniforms for a game before the home fans will be October 10 against Virginia Tech."

In the same article, Jennings quoted Stoll as saying Wake would use a short passing game because "our linemen don't have the size to hold the opponents out for more than a second and a half." Stoll concluded the interview by telling Jennings he was cautiously optimistic about the future. "Our biggest problem is the schedule (Tennessee, Florida State, Houston, and Nebraska) for all away games."

What Stoll couldn't say, because none of us knew it yet, was that the hell we had been put through that spring had indeed forged us into something special. The iron had been pounded. The steel had been crafted. We would face our schedule with an unremitting confidence.

HOPE IN THE
FACE OF DOUBT

Seventy-three players returned to campus in high spirits on August 21 to begin final preparations for the 1970 season. At our opening team dinner, we dined again on London broil, baked potatoes, and salad, followed by ice cream with enough toppings to send us into insulin shock.

The laughter and camaraderie were the same as the year before, but there was a different look to the dining room that evening. We sat as usual in our respective groups with our assistant coaches at the head of each table, but many of us found ourselves eating with a different cohort than in 1969. This was due to Stoll's strategic reshuffling of the team as he fit together the pieces of the puzzle.

Having shown promise at tight end during spring practice. I sat with the receivers, periodically glancing over at the defensive line table and the assistant coach I was so happy to be free of. I gave a thought to wearing my tie-dye scarf but resisted the urge. It would've been inappropriate to disrupt such an upbeat ambience with old grievances.

One of the untold stories about playing football for Wake Forest was the stark reality of returning for summer practice each August. No matter how diligently you jogged or lifted during the off-season, it was never enough preparation for what awaited. This unforgettable suffering is a memory uniquely shared among all Wake Forest football players from the Cal Stoll era.

The first two weeks of summer practice were grueling—three days in shoulder pads and shorts before transitioning to full contact. Hitting again after the long break was a wake-up call. While coaches concerned themselves with conditioning us for the season, our bodies had other ideas. The truth is, jogging uses entirely different muscle tissue than what is needed for firing out at blocking dummies, pushing sleds, or colliding with opposing players. Our hamstrings and glutes received punishing workouts that no amount of off-season training could adequately prepare us for.

This pain-filled ritual might have been manageable except for one architectural challenge: our locker room was located on the ground floor of Reynolds Gymnasium, while the entrance sat two flights above—each with twenty steep steps. After those initial practices, we clung desperately to the railings, moaning audibly as we literally pulled ourselves, hand over hand, up those damn stairs.

In addition to sore muscles, we also developed a mild case of indigestion courtesy of the annual college football previews and projections for the upcoming season. These came out just after Labor Day. *Playboy Magazine* had summarized our prospects with blunt simplicity: "No offense, No defense, No hope." Adding insult to injury, an anonymous source closely associated with the team threw us under the bus. The same *Playboy* article read, "Remembering last season, one Wake Forest staff member remarked, 'When we were bad, we were probably one of the worst teams in the nation; but when we were good, we approached mediocrity.'"

That quote—from one of our own, no less—was grating and embarrassing, knowing that tens of thousands, perhaps *millions* of college football fans would read it. But once the initial shock wore off, it ceased to matter. We followed the lead of Coach Stoll, who never mentioned it, at least to us. He rose above such trivialities. But even Stoll was human, overheard once at a practice ranting to an assistant, "No offense? No defense? My ass!"

The *Playboy* article's ambush was immediately wrong on two fronts, and by mid-season they would be wrong on all three. To begin with, we had hope in spades. After our taxing spring practices with their merciless scrimmages, we felt strong. We might have all been walking wounded in April, but by the end of August, we were fit, confident, and champing at the bit.

And we had a solid defense. Eight starting defensive lettermen were anchored by 6-foot, 3-inch, 240-pound tackle, Win Headley. Named to the preseason All-ACC team, Win was considered by Stoll to be one of the best defensive tackles in the country.

The other defensive tackle was 6-foot, 5-inch Dick Chulada, whose discipline and dedication had transformed him physically. Dick had dropped some 50 pounds since the spring by skipping breakfast and lunch and eating only a moderate dinner.

We had experienced, hard-nosed linebackers in 6-foot, 2-inch, 225-pound Ed Bradley, the scrappy and fearless 5-foot, 11-inch, 190-pound Eddie Stetz, and 6-foot, 1-inch, 215-pound Carlyle Pate.

Our quick and experienced secondaries, Dick Bozoian, Terry Kuharchek, and Pat McHenry, provided solid coverage on passing plays. They also weren't afraid to come up and support against the run.

If we had a weakness, it was on offense. Our offensive line was both small and inexperienced by Division I college football standards. Our two tackles, Tom Martin, at 6 feet, 1-inch, 205 pounds, and 6-foot, 220-pound Vince Nedimyer, had both played guard in 1969. Behind them and pushing for a starting position was Gerry McGowan, who, at 6 feet, 5 inches, and 245 pounds, offered a bit more heft. All three were quick, and quickness would be an asset if Stoll could refine the play-calling to take advantage of a talented group of running backs.

Ken Garrett was lightning fast, having run a 9.6-second 100-yard dash. He was so unusually quick that when he first arrived, our quarterbacks could not execute clean handoffs because he got to them so early. Ken's talent allowed us to run both inside and out. Larry Hopkins, our leading rusher in spring scrimmages, could run inside, outside, and over the top of defenders if need be. Gary Johnson was a former Wisconsin high school hurdle champion who now brought graceful athleticism to our backfield. The returning Steve Bowden was a multiple threat who could easily play flanker, fullback, or split end, giving our offense's versatility.

The receivers, a group I was thrilled to be a part of after my position change, were strong. Our leader was Gary Winrow, entering his third year. His sure hands had bailed out our quarterbacks numerous times. Sophomore Mike Howlette was coming into his own with lightning speed, and by the end of spring practice, he and Junior Moore gave us legitimate deep threats.

After the 1969 season, Cal Stoll had taken stock of where we stood as a program. Despite his eternal optimism, he had always known the season would turn out the way it did. Naturally he never told us that, but his insufferable drills had instilled in us a quiet confidence that allowed us to be beaten badly yet go into the next game full of hope and with enough toughness to withstand the frustration of it all.

We might have lost seven games in 1969, but we looked at 1970 as the year we would turn things around. The criticism stung, but it also served to solidify our resolve. We were more than statistics on a page or standings in a newspaper, and we were dead set on proving it.

That was Stoll's major coup in a season that was best forgotten: He had planted the seeds of belief. It was our job to make them grow.

THE QUARTERBACK DILEMMA

I n 1969, Stoll had nothing to do with the team he inherited from Bill Tate. He made the most of what he had, and the team had shown some promise in our three victories. But now, entering his second season, his influence would be evident in every aspect of the program.

He also knew 1970 would be different in that he would have a hand in both the players he'd use and how he used us. He knew that if we managed to win only three games again, the blame would rest with him.

In a rare show of public introspection with Mary Garber in January, Stoll had said, "Football is a game of men, not systems." This aphorism guided his approach to rebuilding our team. He had spent the spring and summer selecting most of his men, moving us around based on our strengths, rather than forcing us into preestablished roles. Centers became guards, guards became tackles, defensive backs became running backs, and in my case, a defensive end became a tight end. He'd also recruited a great class of junior college transfers, injecting immediate talent and experience into key positions.

But even as we prepared for the Nebraska game, there was one glitch: The ever-assertive Stoll was still unsure as to which system we'd use on offense: a long passing game or an option offense. In 1970, he had two quarterbacks with the skills to do one or the other, but neither was capable of both.

In January, looking back at the 1969 season, Stoll had told Garber, "We didn't have the passer, and we didn't have the big blocking line to be a passing team." In many ways we had been round pegs pounded into square holes, too small and too slow to use the three-back offense that called for a quick and big offensive line to open holes and allow for fast, hard-hitting backs to soften up defenses for the long ball.

By the time we suited up for our first game in Lincoln, most of the questions Stoll faced had been answered. Only one remained, and it was a big one. As we boarded our chartered plane for the long flight to Nebraska, we still did not know which quarterback he would use.

The running, left-handed Larry Russell and the drop-back passer Jim McMahen were still competing for the starting position, each bringing very different skills to the table. After our last scrimmage before the season began, Stoll announced to Garber, "It's still a tie."

A darting and deceptive runner with the reflexes and prescience to see openings before they appeared, Russ's long passes tended to float, becoming open invitations for interceptions. However, he had also demonstrated in 1969 that he could take a hit and bounce back up.

On the other hand, the tall, slender Jim McMahen could throw the long ball with ease, but he lacked Russ's quickness and running agility. And at 6 feet, 2 inches, and 175 pounds, there were doubts about his chances to remain in one piece if he took a hit as a runner.

A two-and-a-half-hour scrimmage on August 29 provided a perfect snapshot of Stoll's dilemma. Russell and McMahen each took turns running the offense for twenty plays before stepping aside for his competitor.

Russ threw the short pass well and, as always, showed his adeptness as a running option quarterback, scoring three times on short bursts after he had driven his team inside the 20-yard line, prompting Stoll to note, "It was his best day since the fall."

Meanwhile, Jim threw touchdown passes of fifty and seventy yards to Gary Winrow and Mike Howlette. "He seems capable of hitting for the long score at any spot at any time, something Wake Forest has lacked," Mary Garber noted in her coverage of the scrimmage.

But Jim had trouble on his exchanges from center, fumbling twice. He also bobbled the ball after being hit hard while dropping back for a pass. "His rushing stats were not impressive," wrote the ever-tactful Garber.

Even after the long scrimmage, Stoll needed more time to finalize the QB situation, which would dictate our offensive system once and for all. "Russell showed he can throw, but he is our running quarterback. We passed more with McMahen at quarterback because we will throw with him. We want each quarterback to do what he does best," Stoll said.

Garber also assessed our running game. "There is little question that the top runner of the day was Larry Hopkins. The fullback from Lee McRae had 178 yards on 18 carries. He runs hard with a kind of speed that gets him to the hole quickly, and he runs over people."

I played in that preseason scrimmage despite having missed all of summer practice due to a bulging disc that had intruded on my sciatic nerve. Three days in the hospital in full-body whirlpools brought little improvement, but with time, the pain gradually lessened to the point where I could stand, then walk, and finally run.

By the end of summer practices, Doc had cleared me to play, so I let Coach Stoll know I would be "ready to go" for our season opener on September 13 against Nebraska in Lincoln. Since I hadn't practiced with the team at all up to that point—and Stoll being a "show-me" kind of guy—he responded that I needed to take part in our final preseason practice scrimmage or stay home. I was more than happy to oblige; I would have done anything to have a chance to play. I participated in the scrimmage and ended up making four catches, enough to get me a seat on the plane to Lincoln.

As we undressed in the locker room after the scrimmage, I turned to several teammates and said, "You know, it feels good to get hit again." That was the wrong thing to say to guys who had been battered continuously during the summer practices I had missed. The locker room fell silent for a split second before a barrage of wadded-up tape balls came flying in my direction.

"Easy for you to say!" someone shouted from across the room. They rode me unmercifully the rest of the day, a reminder that the bonds of brotherhood cut both ways.

LIGHT AT THE END
OF THE TUNNEL

Friday afternoon we gathered for a light practice on Nebraska's newly refurbished field to loosen up and get a feel for the Astroturf. I found the artificial surface intriguing. Making cuts would be easier, but I was somewhat dubious about the unforgiving surface. I knew taking a hit would have consequences. To ease my mind, I tried not to think too much about all the hits we'd be taking.

Talking to reporters after practice, Coach did his best to manage expectations. "I'd be foolish to think we have the personnel to match Nebraska, but you never know about a football game, especially an opener," Stoll said. "We might put it all together tomorrow. They might be a little overconfident."

We could only hope.

The next day, as we entered sold-out Memorial Stadium, it felt like being thrown to the lions in The Roman Colosseum. It was easy to see why the stadium, nicknamed the "Sea of Red," has a reputation as one of the most intimidating venues in American football. To a person, Cornhusker fans were dressed in bright Nebraska Scarlet, enthusiastically waving red flags and pennants. And if the crowd of more than 66,000 wasn't unnerving enough, Nebraska's 180-member band, ninety-player roster, and huge coaching staff only reinforced the feeling that we were David about to face Goliath.

That's not to say there weren't any Demon Deacon fans among the crowd. We were blessed to have a regular and rabid group of supporters who attended every game, home or away, including my parents. No matter where we played, my teammates and I knew we could look into the stands for support and inspiration.

Most of our fans accompanied us to away games, even when we flew. Seeing as we only traveled with forty-seven players, there was plenty of room on the plane. On that particular weekend, more than half the squad was made up of sophomores or junior transfers, traveling to their first away game as a Wake Forest Deacon.

With Stoll's decision on what offense we'd use still weeks away, my participation was limited to specialty teams, kickoffs, kickoff returns, punts, and extra points. Stepping onto the field in front of a deafening mob of Nebraska fans was nothing short of mind-blowing. I suddenly understood the meaning of "home-field advantage."

Nebraska's offense marched onto the field locked and loaded. Despite Coach Stoll's optimism, the only shred of overconfidence the Huskers exhibited came on its very first drive, when a fumble on their own 26-yard line led to a Tracy Lounsbury field goal and a 3-0 lead for us.

Our lead was short-lived. Starting with their next possession, Nebraska monopolized the ball, scoring twice in each of the first two quarters. Their quarterback was 6-foot, 2-inch, 215-pound Jerry Tagge, who later played three years for the Green Bay Packers. His 61-yard touchdown pass to wide receiver and future Heisman Trophy winner Johnny "The Jet" Rodgers—at that time only a sophomore—had all the trappings of an NFL highlight reel.

Meanwhile, their 6-foot, 195-pound halfback Joe Orduna ran for two touchdowns. He also went on to the NFL, playing three seasons with the New York Giants and Baltimore Colts.

Defensively, the Cornhuskers were no less impressive. Our offensive line, still a work in progress, was powerless against their bigger, faster lineman. Every time quarterback Larry Russell attempted a break, he was gang-tackled to the Astroturf. From the sideline, I cringed again and again as Russ was sacked under a swarm of Nebraska jerseys. Between the Huskers' bulldozer-like tackles and the hardness of the Astroturf, we were destined to be mincemeat by the time the game ended.

As the game progressed, all I could think of was Stoll's "pound iron to make steel." If Coach's mantra held any kernel of truth, the powerful Cornhuskers were proving themselves malevolent blacksmiths.

Nebraska dominated the first three quarters. Then, in the fourth quarter, the proverbial weathervane turned in our favor. Both teams pulled their quarterbacks. Having completed nine of twelve passes for 168 yards, Jerry Tagge sat out the fourth quarter on the Huskers' bench. Meanwhile, Stoll sidelined a battered Larry Russell. He was not getting enough protection to work in his running game, and he had made only six of eleven passes for short yardage.

In Russ's place, Stoll inserted Jim McMahen, who, on his first possession, completed six of seven passes to Winrow and Bowden in a 62-yard drive to the goal line. McMahen consummated the drive with a 12-yard touchdown pass to Gary Johnson. Lounsbury kicked the extra point, capping our total points at twelve versus our opponents' thirty-six. In our minds, that fourth quarter represented a small but significant victory: We held them scoreless while earning seven points and, statistically at least, came out ahead.

Stoll's postgame assessment to the press revealed his thoughts. "There are two types of losses. One is the complete mismatch, which tends to destroy your confidence. In the other type, you reflect upon your defeat and decide that if you had done things better, you had an opportunity to win the ball game. Our loss to Nebraska was of the second type."

Our game with Nebraska, a team packed with prime players who had been recruited by football powerhouses, was an obvious mismatch. No one expected us to win. But there were reasons to hope. Against one of the top defensive teams in the country, our offense showed—albeit against their second string—brilliance and scoring power.

On defense, linebackers Carlyle Pate, Ed Bradley, and Eddie Stetz combined for twenty-eight tackles. Defensive tackle Mike Magnot had seven. Tracy Lounsbury averaged forty-two yards per punt against the wind and kicked a field goal and an extra point.

Gary Johnson, courtesy of an aggressive quick-kick call from Stoll, boomed the ball seventy-two yards downfield, pinning Nebraska deep in their own territory. Pat McHenry's block of Nebraska's punt from their own end zone gave us a rare two-point safety.

Steve Bowden caught five passes, indicating he had made a successful switch from running back to wide receiver. Gary Winrow was Gary Winrow, reliable down the stretch that led to our fourth-quarter touchdown.

An unintimidated Larry Hopkins turned heads. "He went into those big Nebraska defensive men with every ounce of his energy, and even as they hauled him down, he was digging for that extra inch," Stoll said after the game.

"I saw a lot of encouraging signs on the field today," Stoll told reporters. "We could have used the fact that we were outmanned as an excuse, but we didn't. Before today, I didn't know what kind of team we would have. Now I'm more confident than ever, and it will be a good one."

Two questions remained: Russell or McMahen? The long ball or the option? It would take another game to find out. We'd gotten our asses whipped, but as we filed onto the plane for the journey home, a modicum of optimism prevailed. The return flight had none of the somberness of other rides home after defeats. Despite the lopsided score, we were close to giddy about what we had done in Lincoln. It was an unusual reaction, and one that made us feel good about our future prospects.

We had stood in the shadow of a team that would become national champions and found something valuable: our fighting spirit. Sometimes, even in defeat, you discover what you're made of. We could finally see a light at the end of the tunnel, and for the first time in recent memory, it wasn't an oncoming train.

HISTORY REPEATS ITSELF

ake Forest and South Carolina had met in football every year since 1938, in a series that dated back to 1909. The Gamecocks led by a slim margin, 21-19-2, with the Deacons last winning in 1968. As freshmen, ten of us had played against South Carolina's freshmen squad: myself, Larry Russell, Archie Logan, Dick Bozoian, Dick Chulada, Gary Winrow, Terry Kuharchek, Mike Magnot, Vince Nedimyer, and Win Headley. In that matchup, we were humiliated 43-7 by the bigger, more disciplined Gamecocks.

Three years later, more disciplined, seasoned, and experienced, we expected to prevail this time. As did Coach Stoll. "We will play better than we did last week," Stoll assured members of the Sportsman's Club at its mid-week luncheon in Winston-Salem. "We are going down there to win, and I think we have a great opportunity to."

Upbeat after our promising fourth quarter against Nebraska, we enjoyed a productive week of practice in preparation for our first ACC contest. Coach Stoll planned to deploy both his quarterbacks, continuing his experimental two-quarterback system.

He cautioned club members, however, that a win in Columbia was not a foregone conclusion. "South Carolina is bigger than Nebraska, and they are as good or better defensively as Nebraska.

"If anything can be gained from losing to Nebraska, our biggest gain was in our confidence," Stoll added. "We lined up against a good football team, and we gave them a good account of ourselves."

Still mired in indecision about whether to start Larry Russell or Jim McMahen at quarterback against South Carolina, he told reporter Mary Garber that, after studying films of the Nebraska game, Wake Forest had "two number-one quarterbacks."

"Our game plan will decide the starter for the game with South Carolina," he explained, "and no matter which man starts, both of them will play."

There was an infallible logic to Stoll's decision. McMahen, in his brief appearance against Nebraska, had led the Deacons 62 yards downfield for a touchdown with pinpoint passing. Russell, though he had no chance to break free in the Nebraska game, had shown in 1969 his breathtaking ability as a running quarterback, something McMahen did not offer.

But if one looked closer, one could see flaws in Stoll's blueprints. Against Nebraska, neither quarterback was able to run effectively, an essential element to either an option offense or one that favors the long ball. In fact, both men ended the Nebraska game with rushing deficits. Russell ran eighteen times, gaining 42 yards but losing 45. McMahen carried twice and lost 11 yards.

Before the game, the always upbeat Stoll was adamant that we would win in Columbia. During practices that week, he made sure we were drilled not to repeat the mistakes we had made in Lincoln. Speaking to Mary Garber, he rattled off a litany of offensive errors in the Nebraska game that we planned to correct against South Carolina: Our timing was off. We missed blocking assignments because we failed to read the defense correctly. Defensively, we had to improve our pass rush and tackling.

When we stepped out onto the field under the Carolina Stadium lights in front of 42,000 Gamecock fans, it was 92 degrees with 82 percent humidity. The air was so dense it felt like trying to breathe through a wet blanket. Slippery with sweat, the balls had to be wiped down and replaced after every change of possession.

Early in the first quarter, after a superb fake from Larry Russell set him free, Larry Hopkins raced 61 yards for a touchdown, weaving through the outstretched arms of off-balance defenders. One reporter called Hoppy's score a "snake dance." The Gamecocks roared back with a touchdown and a field goal.

Down 10-7 at the half, we were within striking distance.

The heat was still so stifling at halftime we met on picnic tables outside the stadium instead of in the locker room. The humid air offered little relief but was better than suffocating in the 100-degree sweat-box in which visiting teams were expected to convene. Meanwhile, South Carolina sought respite in their air-conditioned locker room.

The Gamecocks boasted thirty-six returning lettermen and hadn't lost a home game the previous year. Bigger both offensively and defensively, they also had significantly more depth—fresh bodies to throw at our exhausted lineup. And while we felt, at three points down, that we were still in the game, they were obviously upset with their performance in the first half and eager to redeem themselves.

Our epiphany after the Nebraska game, that we were about to put our losing ways behind us, lasted only minutes into the second half. South Carolina, the defending Atlantic Coast Conference champions and ranked nineteenth in the early 1970 polls, did not get the memo announcing our recent resurgence.

In a display of power and endurance we sadly could not match, the Gamecocks scored thirty-two unanswered points in the second half. Our offense was ineffective. We fumbled, committed numerous penalties, and, in effect, sleepwalked through the second half as if in a trance. South Carolina ran ninety-four plays against our exhausted defense, a number that reflected their dominance and our inability to get them off the field.

Neither of our quarterbacks performed well—not in running, and not in passing. McMahen threw two interceptions and Russell again could not break free in his typical scampering fashion. The Gamecocks pounded us to the point that neither Russ nor Jim had a chance to showcase his strengths. And the rest of us didn't fare much better. The defending ACC champs annihilated us 43-7, the very same score as our freshman game three years earlier.

Mary Garber described the dynamics with piercing accuracy. "Playing against a man who outweighs you by 20 pounds is tough at any time. It is even tougher when the weather is hot, as it was Saturday night. It is tougher when the team you were playing against can keep sending in substitutes."

Granted anonymity, a Wake Forest player described his second half to Garber in terms that captured what we had all experienced. "I did well against the first guy I played against. He was a little bigger, but not much, and I was fine. And I held my own against the second guy, too, though I knew I wasn't quite as fast. But when they sent in a third man against me, I just couldn't handle him. He wasn't as good as the first two, but he was rested."

It was a frustrating, draining experience, especially considering our recently ignited hopes. In our first two games, we were 0-2 and had fumbled seven times, thrown four interceptions, and been called for fourteen costly penalties. The statistics told a story of a team that was its own worst enemy.

We were thoroughly drained after South Carolina, so much so that Stoll allowed us to practice Tuesday in shorts and T-shirts—an unusual concession that acknowledged the physical toll the game had taken. Our bodies were battered, our confidence was shaken, and we had to prepare for yet another challenging opponent.

Up next at Doak Campbell Stadium in Tallahassee was Florida State, a big football school that had compiled a 6-3-1 record in 1969. It would be another profitable game for the coffers of Wake Forest's athletic department, but not necessarily one to put us on the winning streak we desperately wanted, especially given that we'd be subjected to the same outrageous temperatures and humidity that wilted us in South Carolina. On the bright side, the Seminoles showed signs of vulnerability. In their first two games, they had barely beaten Louisville 9-7 and lost to Georgia Tech by ten points.

Stoll announced that Larry Russell would start, perhaps a sign his dual quarterback offense was about to end. I, for one, hoped so. A triple-option offense meant more playing time for me—a selfish, but honest, thought from a player looking for a chance to contribute.

But no matter what offense Stoll finally settled on, our game would not improve until we stopped beating ourselves. The fumbles, the interceptions, the penalties—these self-inflicted wounds had to be addressed before we could hope to compete at the level we aspired to.

We were underdogs going into the game against Florida State, but we took a small bit of comfort knowing that one advantage of being a perpetual underdog is that it makes victory that much sweeter. And despite the disappointment in Columbia, we believed with every fiber of our being that victory would come.

THE VEER

Larry Hopkins' brazen, twisting, 61-yard touchdown run in the first half against South Carolina was not only an exquisite example of his potential; it signaled a watershed moment for us as a team. Hoppy's run was created by Larry Russell. Russ's stealthy handoff confused a pack of South Carolina rushers and sprang Hoppy, allowing him a small opening to break free.

A well-executed option play is a wonder to behold. Conversely, a poorly run one can make everyone involved look like the Keystone Kops. Implementing the triple-option, or "veer," offense called for a few minor changes to our offense, all of which played to our strengths while mitigating our weaknesses. It required that our offensive line be packed tightly—that is, no spreads—thereby negating our opponent's usual speed advantage. The tight line also meant none of our lighter linemen would have to block more than one man at the point of attack, which took away the opposing line's edge in size and strength. Because of that tightness, we often had a spare player available for double teams. That, in turn, created small seams for our backs to take advantage of. Soon enough, we were gaining four or five yards a carry.

Russ's handoff to Hoppy was not a fluke. He was a master at momentarily halting oncoming linemen intent on wreaking havoc on Russell or Hopkins, or both. On paper, the handoff is a simple exchange that, for the most part, goes unnoticed, but it is crucial to nearly every play. A good handoff does not bring the crowd to its feet. There are no statistics on handoffs completed or missed. Good handoffs do not get a quarterback into the NFL.

But Russ's skill, so refined and subtle, bought time. His adeptness in masking where the ball was going took the pressure off our small offensive line. His darting movements after he got the ball from the center created gaps for Hoppy, Ken Garrett, or Gary Johnson to escape through.

But there was more. Fake a handoff, and the field opens up. Russ could then quickly pull back the ball and either run, pitch out, or whip a quick pass on the run. The options, though, depend on the skill of the quarterback to read the action in front of him and react instantly, something Russ was able to do with incredible accuracy.

Russ was the football equivalent of a sidewalk hustler raking in good money with a well-run game of Three Card Monte. When he was on, no one was sure where the ball was until it was too late. You could almost hear the defense groan when they realized they'd been duped again.

Russ was left-handed at a time when left-handed quarterbacks were rare, which made his artistry even more valuable: His movements were unorthodox to rushing linemen or linebackers. Plus, at 5 feet, 11 inches, he was smaller than most Division I quarterbacks, which only furthered his magic. His quickness was extraordinary.

Very few people who followed college football knew about Russell, a function of his playing for Wake Forest in the ACC. But he was one of the best option quarterbacks in the country. His was a unique talent, custom-made for the veer offense.

We had the two Larrys—Russell and Hopkins—and we had the supporting players needed to make the most of Russ's ability to run the option. The triple threat of backs Hoppy, Ken Garrett, or Gary Johnson breaking through the opposing defensive front seven for long runs allowed our receivers to get open for short, quick passes over the middle or cuts to the sideline. In essence, we did not need the long ball.

Once we began running the veer, Wake Forest stuck to the ground game almost exclusively. Running on his own, Russ gained 649 yards and scored 10 touchdowns in 10 games while completing only 109 passes. Every other play was a handoff, because that was where our strength lay.

Assistant coach Oval Jaynes recalls, "I don't remember Russell ever missing a play. He was the toughest kid you've ever seen and quick as a hiccup." His words capture not just Russ's skill, but his grit and reliability that formed the basis of our offensive identity.

In 1970, Hopkins led all Wake Forest rushers with just under 1,000 yards and was named first-team All ACC. Meanwhile, Garrett and Johnson rotated in the other running back slot, creating a three-headed rushing attack that kept defenses guessing.

With Russell running the option, defenders were forced to guess which running back had the ball. That split second of unpredictability made all the difference. For our ends and flankers, it meant openings for short passes. But more than anything, the veer meant our offense could slowly work its way downfield, eating up the clock and providing much-needed rest for our defense. Ideally, our defense would return to the field refreshed after a protracted and hopefully productive drive.

Fresh defensive legs were a precious commodity. We had little depth, and it showed against South Carolina: Fatigue took over our muscles and minds in the fourth quarter. Speaking to Mary Garber after our loss to the Gamecocks, Stoll said, "It all goes back to a basic premise of football. It is more difficult to concentrate when you are tired, and it is important for a football player to make himself concentrate when he is tired."

The veer also meant there was no longer a need to take chances with a long pass. By keeping the ball close on offense, we could control the game. This system frustrates the defense, leading to mistakes in coverage.

Gary German, our rangy center, described the rationale for transitioning to the veer. "I was the perfect size for a wide receiver or defensive back. The trouble was that I was an offensive lineman, a center. I was exceedingly small for the position. To make matters worse, I was one of our bigger guys."

Gary continued. "We started the season with an offense that we called a 'pro-spread attack.' The idea was to spread the defense across the field and make the other team chase us." He then explained why that tactic did not work. "We might have been small, but we were slow, too. When we challenged people to catch us, they did."

Stoll saw the flaws too. At Monday's practice after our loss to South Carolina, he called us together and said, "Boys, throw away your playbooks. We need a new offense, preferably one that does not require size, speed, or athleticism."

The laughter that followed masked the serious intent behind our coach's words. We needed change, and we needed it fast.

PIECING IT
TOGETHER

In the week leading up to the Florida State game, Coach Stoll made sure we knew that the Seminoles were picked to win by fifteen points. He had talked to former Wake assistant Tom Moore, now coaching at Georgia Tech. His team had just played Florida. Moore told Stoll he thought Florida State was stronger than South Carolina. The odds against us in Tallahassee were nothing new. The bookmakers had dismissed us before we even arrived, which only fueled our determination to prove them wrong.

Prior to the Florida State game, Stoll's announcement to the press about our new offense was easily the most abridged description of the complicated veer ever given. He told reporters before the game, "We will be making some changes in our offense. Larry Russell will start, and we will use short passes to our tight ends and backs to put some pressure on their linebackers."

Against the Seminoles, we planned to use the veer offense for the first time, with Gary Winrow and myself as the two tight ends, Steve Bowden at wide receiver, and the talented trio of Larry Russell, Larry Hopkins, and Gary

Johnson in the backfield. I benefited greatly from this new system, starting regularly as the weakside tight end.

The veer made the most of our offense by not requiring our smaller offensive lineman to go head-to-head with much bigger linemen or linebackers for extended periods of time. They only needed to protect Russell long enough for him to option the ball to a running back, scramble while looking for an open receiver downfield, or tuck the ball and run.

Veer or no veer, we were not at full strength. The speedy Ken Garrett, still nursing a sore ankle, was temporarily limited to kickoff and punt returns. In addition, offensive tackle Vince Nedimyer and defensive lineman Dick Chulada were both sidelined with injuries.

Despite not having all our starters, we had an outstanding first half. There were many reasons to be encouraged, the first being that our nascent veer offense was starting to have an effect "by using quick-opening plays, which were cleverly set up and veiled by Larry Russell, a junior quarterback," as recorded in *The Tallahassee Democrat*. The *Winston-Salem Journal* also noted Russ's prowess, "Quarterback Larry Russell executed some triple option plays with keen finesse."

We picked up 239 yards on the ground and had nine runs of at least 10 yards. Gary Johnson rushed for 110 yards and Hopkins for 71. Garrett, despite his sore ankle, returned three kickoffs for 92 yards. The foot of punter Tracy Lounsbury forced the Seminoles to start each drive from deep in their own territory.

We went into the locker room up 14-6 at the half feeling pretty good. When we came out, however, our offense imploded. Larry Lyon of the *Old Gold & Black* wryly recalled the main problem. "Whoever designed the football over 100 years ago left off one thing that the current Wake Forest gridders need badly: a handle. For without it, the Deacs are finding it very hard to hold on to that peculiarly shaped ball that they are unfortunately required to play with. In Tallahassee, Wake was sitting on top of a 14-6 margin over Florida State at intermission, and they were thinking glorious thoughts of an upset and victory number one in 1970. They would have had that upset if it wasn't for one thing: they began to cough up the football with regularity in the final half."

Despite the alarming number of Wake Forest turnovers in the second half, outstanding play by our defense kept us alive until the fourth quarter. Eddie

Stetz, Carlyle Pate, and Win Headley provided what the *Winston-Salem Journal* termed "a savage defense," allowing only one touchdown. The Seminoles' other thirteen points all came off the bare foot of Frank Fontes, a 5-foot, 6-inch, soccer-style placekicker. Originally from North Africa, Fontes had played high school football in Northern Virginia. He made four field goals of 39, 22, 47, and 37 yards and missed four more attempts from 32, 46, 53, and 30. He also kicked the extra point after the Seminoles' lone TD. Final score: Florida State 19, Wake Forest 14.

We came gut-wrenchingly close to an upset on September 26, but close, as the saying goes, only counts with horseshoes and hand grenades. "Our game plan was super," Cal Stoll told reporters as we prepared to head home. "But it wasn't in the game plan to fumble. Florida State didn't stop us. We stopped ourselves. Our defense played well, but they were in there too long again."

In a separate *Old Gold & Black* piece, Larry Lyon drew attention to one of our defensive standouts who kept us in the game. "Terry Kuharchek is a relatively unknown and unsung senior who is currently starting as the Deacs safety for the third straight year and who is, according to Coach Stoll, 'perhaps the best safety man in the conference.' Besides leading Wake in interceptions last season with four, the 6-foot, 1-inch, 190-pounder was in on over 70 tackles, one of the top marks on the team."

Lyon then went on to quote Terry. "The first goal is to win the conference. We can still do it now since it's early in the season," Terry said. "I think that team morale is still high, but the team needs to concentrate more when we're tired, and since we don't have the depth, the regulars have to give 100%."

The Florida State loss prompted us to do something we'd never done—call for a players-only meeting when we arrived back in Winston-Salem. In the meeting, Terry and other team leaders talked to us about goals. We didn't know it then, but that seminal conversation would determine the outcome of our season.

LETTING
US RUN

The week before the Virginia game, things were not looking so rosy. As usual, we were predicted to lose, this time by seven points. Stoll, of course, told the weekly gathering at the Sportsman's Club he was confident we would beat the Cavaliers. He always said that. Whether he believed it or not is a question better left unanswered.

At the midweek luncheon, he briefly touched on a few concerns. Key players were out with injuries, and our experimental veer offense was yet unproven. We had shot ourselves in the foot in Tallahassee, and the coaching staff was not totally convinced the veer was the answer.

In addition, our lack of depth made losing even one starter a serious concern. Gary Winrow and Ken Garrett were recovering from ankle injuries and were questionable. Carlyle Pate was out. Gary Johnson was hobbled by a charley horse.

Stoll had other reasons to be nervous. Using the veer against Virginia meant last-second handoffs and pitchouts. Having fumbled the ball four times against Florida State, we had not exactly convinced offensive coordinator Oval Jaynes that we had the new system under control.

Stoll touched on the fumbles only briefly—in jest. He told his Sportsman's Club audience he had appointed himself "head fumble coach." Every back, flanker, and end in practice that week who had any chance of touching the ball in the Virginia game had it drummed into his head to use three points of contact when we had the ball—our hands, our elbows, and our forearms. "If you do that, it is impossible to drop the ball," Stoll told us. Then he said it again.

There was another concern: Virginia's unorthodox defense. After viewing game films of UVA, Wake Forest coaches knew the Cavaliers' defensive sets were unpredictable. Virginia used a basic 4-3 defense, four men in the front line and three linebackers, but they rarely stuck to it. The big problem for Wake Forest, according to Jaynes, was that Virginia's defensive unit constantly changed their alignment at the line of scrimmage. They sometimes moved all eleven men close to the line of scrimmage, and they stunted about 85 percent of the time—linemen and linebackers changing their point of attack just before the snap.

This presented a challenge on two fronts. First, to Larry Russell, who had to quickly read the defense when choosing the option, and second, to our offensive line, because stunting requires changing blocking assignments at the last second. "It's hard to set up a game plan because there does not seem to be any pattern in Virginia's defensive moves. It will come down to a guessing game," Jaynes told Mary Garber. "We'll try to guess what they are going to do. If we guess right, we could get a long gain. If we guess wrong, we could have no gain or be thrown for a loss."

An *Old Gold & Black* piece captured the prevailing mood around campus. "Wake Forest versus Virginia. Doesn't sound very important. Does it? To the vast majority of football fans, it isn't. After all, isn't this the one that they are calling the Cellar Bowl? The winner will probably finish in seventh place—the loser in the ACC basement. Surely, no one can really get excited about WFU versus UVA on the same Saturday North Carolina is trying to remain unde-feated, Duke is attempting to upset the number one-ranked Buckeyes of Ohio State, and NC State is seeking a prestigious win against Florida. Undoubtedly, very few people will treat the outcome of tomorrow's Wake versus Virginia contest with a little more than a 'ho-hum.' But if you have any interest in Deacon football, you cannot avoid the fact that this is not just another game for Cal Stoll's contingent."

Stunting or no stunting, there was no guessing that day. Larry Russell played with clairvoyance. No matter what defense Virginia threw at him, they had no answers to his rollouts, pitches, and tuck-and-runs. Instead of making mistakes, we seized control.

Everything came together. Our veer offense kicked in, and I was elated to have an active role. Early in the first quarter, Russ reeled off a 20-yard run to the Virginia 30. On the next play, he rolled out right as I blocked an onrushing safety to spring him for a 30-yard sprint into the end zone. It went that way all afternoon, each position playing his role to perfection.

Russell scored two rushing touchdowns and passed to Ken Garrett for a third. Tracy Lounsbury added three extra points and two field goals. Pat McHenry intercepted a pass on our 40-yard line and broke 23 yards to Virginia's 38. Three plays later, Lounsbury kicked a field goal just before the half. We went into the locker room ahead 20-0, a vastly different scenario than halftime in Lincoln or Columbia.

McHenry grabbed another interception in the second half. Russell, Garrett, and Hopkins ran at will. We picked up 271 yards on the ground, getting a large chunk of it from Russell, who ran for 121 yards on 21 carries, and Garrett, free from his nagging ankle injury for the first time that season, who gained 64 yards on 16 attempts. Hopkins added another 57 yards. Meanwhile, our defense gave the Cavaliers little chance to come up for air, with three interceptions and two fumble recoveries in the first half alone.

As the second half wound down, Virginia's only opportunity at saving face was to avoid a shutout, which they managed by scoring against our second string with 59 seconds left. Stoll emptied the bench, our younger players received valuable game experience, and we walked off victorious.

The *Old Gold & Black* reporter was right on target. This was not "just another game." And we did not simply "beat" Virginia. We embarrassed them 27-7 on their home turf.

The more cynical of our fans might have said our first win of the season against the Orange and Blue was a matter of probability. That, at *some* point, the odds dictated we would beat *someone*. I would argue that the odds of an eventual win, lady luck, or Stoll's oft-used "bounce of the ball," whatever you want to call it, had nothing to do with the outcome. Our first win had everything to do with us making our own luck. Good fortune might have come along for the ride, but we were driving the bus.

Winning in such spectacular fashion was sublime, and there were signs we would not have to wait another year for the next one. That afternoon, we had an offense, a defense, and, more than anything, hope.

For Cavalier fans, the loss was disheartening. The *Charlottesville Daily Progress* offered a grim assessment. "There were a lot of University of Virginia alumni who returned to Charlottesville Saturday afternoon to see the Cavaliers play Wake Forest. Most of them didn't get to see much, at least much that was worth the long trip. The Cavaliers were soundly trounced by the Deacons 27-7. Those who came late missed Wake Forest's 20 points in the first half, and those who left early didn't get to see Virginia's lone score in the last minute of the game. The Deacons were not to be denied. Wake Forest had lost its first three outings of the season despite playing fairly respectable football, and it was charged to the hilt for this one."

Virginia Head Coach George Blackburn spoke to reporters afterward. "I said before this game that Wake is vastly underrated. Now, I guess someone might believe me. Russell really keeps you off balance. He can run and pass, and when he isn't doing something with the ball, he has Garrett to carry it."

Russell was named ACC Offensive Player of the Week for his 121 rushing yards, touchdown pass, and overall dominance of a reeling Virginia defense. "Larry played his best game since he has been at Wake Forest," offensive coordinator Oval Jaynes told reporters. "He kept Virginia off guard all afternoon. They were confused about who had the ball and what we were doing, particularly in the early part of the game. He called a beautiful game, and most of his calls were from the line of scrimmage." That was the veer in its most efficient gear.

As good as our offense was that day, Stoll felt our offense could have done better. "We made a lot of our own breaks early in the game. And we could have been leading by more in the first half, but we've never been in that position since I've been at Wake Forest," he said.

As for our defense, it was impenetrable. Beginning from Virginia's first possession, the Cavaliers were unable to move the ball in any fashion. Terry Kuharchek was named ACC Defensive Back of the Week. He deflected one

Virginia pass that was intercepted by Pat McHenry, recovered a fumble, and set up another Wake Forest touchdown with a 24-yard punt return.

Stoll took time after the game to heap praise on the efforts of tackle Win Headley. "There is no better defensive tackle in the country," Stoll told reporters. "Every team we played has felt that way about him. He does one heck of a job."

Old Gold & Black sports editor Charlie Dayton summed up the game eloquently. "Despite recent reports to the contrary, Wake Forest is not the worst football team in the country. If any proof of the Demon Deacon's capability is needed, just consult Virginia coach Jerry George Blackburn, who saw his Cavaliers decisively beaten last night 27-7 before a UVA homecoming crowd of 21,500. The Deacs went into the contest, which had been selected as the 'Crummy Game of the Week' in last week's column, as a one-touchdown underdog to the Wahoos. At the game's conclusion, only those stunned Cavalier fans who had gone to Scott Stadium anticipating a Wahoo walk-a-way win would have agreed with the selection.

"For the Deacs, it was the high point of what has been a very frustrating season. In their first three games, Stoll's squad had squandered away the ball in every imaginable way. Although the talent for a solid team seemed to be present, fumbles, penalties, and interceptions repeatedly squelched any sustained Wake efforts. When it was all over, Blackburn was queried about the game and replied, 'The big thing is that Wake Forest is vastly underrated. They're as good a team as we play all year.'"

The victory was as gratifying for our fans as it was for us. As we emerged from Virginia's visitors' locker room, we were greeted by more than two dozen Demon Deacon faithful who had traveled to Charlottesville in hopes of being the first to congratulate us on our first win of the season. Martha "Marty" Hill, Larry Russell's girlfriend, was among them, having driven down from Beaver College, Pennsylvania, where she was a student. Larry went over to Marty and gave her a long hug. They exchanged a few words, and then Larry proceeded to the buses. It was the last time he would see her alive.

28

LIFE'S HARDEST LESSON

The 200-mile drive south back to Winston-Salem after the win in Charlottesville should have been a breeze. There was little to see in the darkness and the rain, and few towns to interrupt our reverie. Our time on the buses before heading back to campus for another week of practice and classes was a rare break. We had three hours to do nothing but relive the game, basking in the exhilaration of our victory. It should have been a party the entire way home, and in the beginning, as we headed home from Charlottesville on VA Route 29, it was.

Though I choose not to, I can bring myself back there in an instant. Every single one of us can. Sitting on the bus, driving through the night, happy, tired, laughing. The hum of the engine beneath us, the rhythmic swish of wipers clearing raindrops from the windshield, the glare of headlights from oncoming cars reflecting on wet pavement. And nothing in our minds but visions of future glory.

About fifteen minutes outside Charlottesville, the traffic slowed. Ahead of us, slightly off the road, a car with Massachusetts' plates lay on its roof.

As we approached the scene of the accident, Larry Russell, sitting in the front seat nearest the door, stood up and started yelling frantically at the driver, "Pull over! Pull over! Open the door! That's Marty's car!"

Mickey Neher was in the seat directly behind Larry. He recalls the scene as if it were yesterday. "The bus came to a stop, and all conversation ceased. The driver opened the door, and Larry raced down the steps and toward the overturned vehicle. The rest of us spent the next few minutes staring anxiously out the bus windows in disbelief. Finally, Vince Nedimeyer stood up, and in a strong voice, commanded us to 'Take a knee and bow your heads.' Then he began to recite the Lord's Prayer: 'Our Father who art in Heaven, hallowed be thy name...' We all joined in. We recited it two—maybe three—times."

How the word spread, how we absorbed what happened, what we did after, is still a blur. We were beyond stunned. Russ's girlfriend, Martha Jean Hill, the young woman in the overturned car, was dead.

She had begun the weekend as we all had, making the drive to Charlottesville for a football game. She had left the stadium after the game as we all did—elated about our win and excited to have witnessed her boyfriend's heroics.

Marty and Larry had known each other for years. They had been high-school classmates in their hometown of Newburyport, Massachusetts, a quintessential New England seaside village close to the New Hampshire border. A place vastly different from the Virginia countryside where her life abruptly ended.

Staring at the droplets of rain on the bus windows, I remember wishing it was all a cruel nightmare I would soon wake up from. Everything that followed—the three-hour ride home, pulling into the parking lot outside Reynolds Gymnasium, grabbing my bag, and heading back to my room—is lost, washed away in the rain and darkness of that terrible night.

I speak for the entire team when I say that the harshest lesson was knowing we could not change a thing. We looked for answers where there weren't any. There was nothing to say, nothing to do. Nothing left but an overwhelming feeling of sadness that enveloped each of us.

The next day, Russ traveled home to Massachusetts for Marty's funeral. He returned four days later for a campus memorial service at Wait Chapel. The entire team showed up. We sat quietly in the pews, unsure what to do or say. We were naive young men, unfamiliar with the customs and rituals surrounding death, especially the death of someone so young.

I remember wishing I did not have to be at a memorial service for a vibrant 20-year-old woman. But I also recall thinking I would not have wanted to be anywhere else. I wanted to show Russ how deeply I cared about him. But like everyone else, I was too young to articulate any meaningful expression of sympathy outside my own muted presence.

For that hour, I sat transfixed, staring down at my folded hands. I can't tell you what the chaplain said, nor anything else about the service. I do know this. The past and future ceased to exist. Football disappeared. Wins and losses became meaningless. And I felt changed—older, yet more like a child than I had felt in a long time. At the same time, I remember feeling oddly comforted that my teammates felt every bit as helpless as I did.

As I think about it now, there are still no answers as to how or why what happened, happened. But back then, we looked to Russ for answers. And being the exceptional leader he was, he provided them.

More dedicated than ever to being a committed and loyal teammate, he announced his intention to play against Virginia Tech. "Marty would have wanted that," he told Mary Garber in a pregame interview. Russ snapped us out of our fog, and we followed his lead. His strength became our strength, his emotional resilience a source of motivation. Confronted with immeasurable tragedy, he showed us the right way to honor the dead—by living fully and continuing to pursue our dreams.

A TRADITION
IS BORN

The win over UVA, especially with its not-even-close, never-a-doubt manner, was exhilarating. Unsaid, though felt by everyone, was that our thumping of the Cavaliers had brought an immediate sense of relief. Ahead lay ACC games with Clemson, the University of North Carolina, Duke, and North Carolina State. With a 1-1 conference record, we were in the hunt for the championship. "It's about time," a relieved Stoll told assembled reporters after the game. "It's been the other way all year."

Along the way, we found something else, a talisman we'd call upon for the rest of the season. Like most athletes, every player on our team had superstitions he looked to before a game, a ritual or touchstone he deemed necessary. Perhaps it was a lucky pair of socks, the order in which he tied his cleats, a particular food that had to be eaten, or possibly an introspective minute to invoke a positive outcome. After the win in Charlottesville, ours became "Simos."

At the beginning of the season, Stoll issued an edict that players were to avoid any local bar frequented by Wake students, such as the Tavern on the Green. But he neglected to say anything about bars *not* frequented by Wake students.

The week before the Virginia game, a few team members took a ride out to Simos Barbeque Inn on Indiana Avenue in Winston-Salem, far from campus. Since it was not the type of watering hole to attract many Wake Forest students, it was ideally situated for slipping under Stoll's radar.

Two graduate assistant coaches had tipped off some Deac players to Simos' delights, which included plenty of beer served in frosty mugs, greasy but delicious burgers and dogs, and, of course, barbecue. Simos was, colloquially speaking, a dive. But to us, it was a safe haven, unlikely to show up on Stoll's *verboten* list.

Wednesday night before the Virginia game, six or so of the more adventurous among us—willing to risk Dawn Patrols if caught—made our way to Simos to enjoy a quiet evening of beer and gut-bomb burgers. It turned out to be the ideal drinking venue. No one knew who the new tableful of young guys was, and better yet, no one cared to know. We drank and ate in anonymity, safely beyond Cal Stoll's metaphorical reach. Three days later, we went out and played the game of our Wake Forest careers.

That Wednesday night a new tradition was born. Word spread among the team, and as we moved into the rest of the season, more players joined in. An evening at Simos became, for many, the best way to prepare ourselves for Saturday.

NOW OR NEVER

Friday before the Virginia Tech game, as we suited up for practice, Russ spoke to us. "If you've ever thought about doing something," he began, "the time to do it is now. You might never get the chance to do it later." He did not have to explain. If Marty's death taught us anything, it's that life carries no guarantees.

The next day, October 11, we were on a one-game winning streak heading into our matchup with Virginia Tech. Unlike our previous game at the University of Virginia, we did not have to board a bus to the airport or anywhere else. We were home among friends and supporters. It was Parents Weekend: The stadium would be filled, and many family members would be there.

We dedicated the game to the memory of Marty Hill, who had cheered for us the week before. It was already planned that when the game ended, win or lose, Coach Cal Stoll would present the game ball to Marty's father, Harry, who had made the long trip down from Newburyport.

All eyes were on Larry Russell. If he played poorly or distractedly, not one of the 18,500 Parents Weekend spectators in Groves Stadium would have blamed him.

We started slowly, appearing lethargic in the first quarter, our offense languid. At the end of the first quarter, we found ourselves down 3-0, the result of a Hokie field goal.

Early in the second quarter, as he scrambled to recover after a broken play, Russ launched a wobbly Hail Mary pass from our own 30-yard line. The ball hung in the air seemingly forever. The intended target, Gary Johnson, saw the projectile coming, oblivious that he was about to be sandwiched by two Virginia Tech defenders. Launching himself skyward, Gary snatched the ball in front of the outstretched hands of a Hokie defensive back before being tackled for a 42-yard gain.

Everyone watching seemed to realize Russ should not have thrown into thick coverage. Johnson, however, had not the slightest idea. "I didn't even know they were there," he said afterward, referring to the defenders. "I thought I was all alone. I thought I could go in for a touchdown."

On the next play, Russ handed off to Larry Hopkins for 5 yards, then held onto the pigskin for back-to-back gains of 18 and 6. After two more handoffs to Hoppy for 7 yards, Russell spotted tight end Gary Winrow in the left flat and threaded a pass to him in the end zone between three defenders.

On the ensuing point-after attempt, a bad exchange as Tracy Lounsbury lined up for the kick hit the ground before it reached Larry Russell, our holder. Unflustered, Russ scooped up the ball and raced to the corner for a two-point conversion, turning a botched point-after attempt into an auspicious gain. We were suddenly up 8-3 with almost three quarters left to play.

From that point on, we never looked back. Our offense continued to fire at will, scoring three times in the second quarter and once in the third. Most of the fourth quarter, however, was played in our own end. Defensive standouts Dick Chulada, Ed Bradley, and Larry Causey stood firm against Virginia Tech's running backs, holding them to a total 143 yards on the ground. They also halted two separate Hokie drives—on the 5- and 11-yard lines—resulting in two field goals but no touchdowns. Final score: Wake Forest 28, Virginia Tech 9.

Dispirited Hokie Head Coach Jerry Claiborne viewed the near interception of Russell's pass to Johnson as the deciding factor in the game. In contrast, we saw it not as a near interception, but as a terrific catch by Gary that highlighted not only his athleticism, but also, how fast we could ignite when the tide began to turn.

"We should have intercepted," Claiborne said. "That play alone could've been the difference in the game. Instead of us having the ball, they had a 42-yard completion, and then they went on to score the go-ahead touchdown. After that, Russell really went to work on us. He did a truly outstanding job of running that option and mixing up his plays." Claiborne also praised our defense. "Every time we got something going, it seemed like either Headley or Stetz would break through and stop the drive," he told reporters.

One-man juggernaut Larry Russell played the game of his young life. Incredible by any measure, his execution was nothing short of surreal given the tragic loss he had just gone through and was still actively grieving.

Old Gold & Black sportswriter Charlie Dayton captured Russ's superhuman effort in an article titled "Year of the Quarterback."

"The shifty signal-caller gained 122 yards rushing as he ran the triple option play like nobody else can, faking and maneuvering his way consistently throughout the befuddled VPI line. Running for two scores on jaunts of 12 and 28 yards, passing for two more to Gary Winrow and Dave Doda, and accumulating 199 yards in total offense. Russell enjoyed his best day ever as a Deacon. The effort surpassed his performance against Virginia a week before that had won him 'ACC Back of the Week' laurels."

Dayton also gave kudos to the quarterback's supporting cast. "While Russell was super, he had a lot of help, both in the back of him and in front. Up front, the blocking of ends Dave Doda and Gary Winrow, tackles Vince Nedimyer and Gerald McGowan, guards Ted Waite and Bill Bobbora, and center Nick Vrhovac was superb, constantly providing daylight for Russell and company. Back of Russell, there was Larry Hopkins, Ken Garrett, and Gary Johnson, who totaled 166 yards rushing between them, with 'Hoppy' getting half of that total. Sophomore Ken Garrett, who seems to be fully recovered from an ankle injury that hampered his running earlier in the season, contributed 64 yards on 16 carries."

After the game, Stoll met with the usual flock of reporters. Coach was neither a gloater nor a man who sought to disparage critics. It is clear, though, that while he never mentioned the many football savants who predicted we would not win a game all season, like an elephant, he never forgot.

"This is a lot better than losing, isn't it?" he said, in his understated style. "I guess this puts us ahead of where most people thought we'd be." Stoll then waxed optimistic about the future. "This team is a helluva lot better than it was a month ago," he told a reporter. "We've got a bunch of young kids, but they've got a whole lot of heart. They are getting the feeling of the game a lot better."

Then he added, as if talking directly to his many detractors, "I have said all this time they would get better. And they have."

Naturally, the press aimed their microphones at Larry Russell. And, as usual, he shrugged it off. "This was the best prepared I have ever been," he said. "I especially wanted to be ready because of last week," he told Mary Garber, alluding to the tragedy on the way home from the Virginia game.

Then he diverted the spotlight and aimed it at his teammates. "The offensive line was great. Gerald McGowan, Ted Waite, Nick Vrhovac, Bill Bobbora, Vince Nedimyer, and Dave Doda, all of them blocked well. They were the ones who did it," Russ said. "I would go down the line and react to the movement of the defense, and when I got to the end, there would be no one standing."

The *Old Gold & Black* game analysis echoed the sentiments of many of Wake Forest's long-suffering fans. "To the average Wake Forest football fan, two wins in a row is a little hard to believe. After all, the Deacs only had three two-game winning streaks in all of the 1960's (excluding that freak of four games at the end of the 1967 season). And when each of those two victories are by margins of three touchdowns, it becomes mind-boggling. It occurs to the average Wake Forest football fan that something must really be happening over on that practice field by Reynolds Gym every afternoon".

Ironically, it was Virginia Tech's coach, Jerry Claiborne, who gave the most succinct and accurate description of the game. As a coach who knew he had lost to a better team, he owned up to the truth. "We had several players hurt during the game, but even if we had been healthy, I don't know if we could've beaten them the way they were playing today."

The way we were playing had a nice feel to it—an unfamiliar, *winning* feel—something that no one wearing the gold and black of Wake Forest that day had experienced before. The scoreboard may have told the story of our dominance, but the wonderous feeling of everything falling into place told so much more. We believed in our coach. We believed in ourselves. And most important of all, we believed in each other.

THE TURNING POINT

Even as we celebrated our victory over Virginia Tech, our upcoming matchup with Clemson loomed large. Energized by our two-game winning streak and how well we were playing, we felt confident we could put the specters of the past to rest. We'd finally gotten the monkey off our backs and were more than happy to hand it over to someone else.

Old Gold & Black sports editor George Wright offered this preview. "The Deacon gridders go after their third win in a row this weekend when they host the Clemson Tigers at Groves Stadium in the 1970 Homecoming game. While the Tigers seem to be playing worse with each week, the Deacons are improving with each passing contest. The Deacons have met the Tigers 35 times in a series that began in 1933. Clemson holds the series edge, having won 25 while losing only nine games."

Head games, if you allow them, can be more exhausting than actually playing football. The weight of expectation, the shadow of past defeats, the cyclical thoughts that keep you up at night—these psychological burdens can sabotage a team's morale before they even take the field.

We tried to avoid such mental traps. But as we began to string together victories, overthinking became inevitable. On October 17, as we dressed in the Groves Stadium Field House, a capacity Homecoming crowd waited outside in anticipation, daring to hope for another win. Yet inside the locker room, an odd mix of emotions prevailed. No player suiting up that afternoon had ever beaten Clemson.

Wake Forest's last win against the Tigers had been in 1961, when most of us were playing Pop Warner football, if we were playing at all. The statistics haunted us: a lopsided 23-6 loss in 1967, a frustrating 20-20 tie in 1968, and a 28-14 thumping in 1969. Recent history was not on our side.

On the other hand, we had a lot going for us. We had more than defeated Virginia and Virginia Tech—we had annihilated them. In both contests, Larry Russell was at the top of his game, the offensive line blocked with near-perfect precision, and our defense was hell-bent on preventing any touchdowns by the opposition. All the gears were meshing perfectly.

Or so we thought. As the game got underway, that old familiar dread threatened to resurface. Our offense, explosive in the previous two games, was slow getting out of the blocks. Early in the first quarter, our star fullback, Larry Hopkins, fumbled on his third carry. Clemson pounced on the ball at their own 45-yard line. Stoll promptly pulled Hoppy from the game and sat him on the bench.

Our other Larry, quarterback Larry Russell, struggled with his reads, the most crucial element of our complicated veer offense. Clemson Head Coach Cecil "Hootie" Ingram had evidently paid attention to the scouting reports, his defense shutting down Russ's options to the outside—normally our best weapon.

From our first possession, Stoll and Ingram engaged in an intricate chess match: Offensive move. Defensive counter. "We had a lot of trouble with our offense at the start of the game," Stoll later explained to reporters. "Larry Russell probably had more bad reads guessing what Clemson's defense would do than he has had in his last three games. Clemson was stopping us from the tackle out at the start. Then we adjusted and started trapping in the middle, and Larry Hopkins finally got us going."

Re-entering the game after a brief exile, Hoppy exploded onto the field like a man possessed. After escaping Coach Stoll's chastening time on the bench, he delivered what one reporter described as "one of the greatest performances ever seen at an Atlantic Coast Conference stadium."

Hopkins didn't just defeat the Tiger defense, he dismantled it completely. If there had ever been any question as to why Stoll had recruited Hoppy, the fans were seeing it now. On his first two carries after returning to the field, Hoppy broke free for gains of 14 and 21 yards, giving us a sample preview of what was to come. In the third quarter, when fatigue typically sets in, he delivered blistering runs of 35 and 23 yards, running around or over any defensive player who dared to get in his way.

In the fourth quarter, when most backs typically show signs of slowing down, he kicked it into high gear with successive runs of 50 and 19 yards, the latter for a touchdown. I witnessed the 50-yarder from an unusual vantage point, flat on the Groves Stadium grass after taking out the safety and springing Hoppy to scamper untouched down the field.

But Hopkins was far from done. He authored another stunning series of breaks: a 24-yard gain followed by rushes of 14 and 20 yards. Then he capped his display of power and agility with a 44-yard dash for a touchdown that left bewildered Tiger defenders grasping at air.

By game's end, Hopkins had set a new ACC single-game rushing record: 230 yards in 20 carries, including two touchdowns. His stats on the day helped set a Wake Forest football record of 444 total yards rushing.

While Hopkins may have commandeered the spotlight, our other backs did more than spectate. Installing the trap block and going inside had indeed yielded fruit, opening up the Clemson defense like a can opener. Russ held onto the ball for a 60-yard gain that brought the crowd to its feet. On the next play, he handed off to Ken Garrett, who ran 28 yards into the end zone.

Our defense, meanwhile, played with unbridled ferocity. Led by a blitzing Ed Bradley, Eddie Stetz, and Win Headley, they flattened Clemson's backs with jarring tackles, accumulating losses of some 55 yards. Bradley alone registered three quarterback sacks.

The Tiger offense appeared completely overwhelmed, managing to move into Deacon territory only once the entire first half. By the final whistle, we had comfortably dispatched Clemson 36-20. Their scores came only in the fourth quarter, while our first-string defense enjoyed a well-deserved rest on the sidelines, and our reserves gleaned benefits from an actual game situation.

An article in the *Old Gold & Black* captured our domination eloquently. "The Deacs blasted the Tigers, 36-20, as Stoll's squad humbled the Tiger defensive unit, rolling up 444 yards rushing and scoring a season-high of 36 points, only eight points less than eighth-ranked Auburn totaled against the Tigers the week before. And the Deacs would have scored more, possibly, if they had not fumbled twice, once on first down at the Clemson one-yard line. The defense had one of its biggest days, too, as they held the Tiger offense scoreless for three quarters. And when the Tigers, playing without the services of All-ACC Ray Yauger, did muster up a scoring threat, it was against the Deacon second stringers."

The article went on to praise the team's overall team effort before singling out the hardworking but oft-overlooked offensive linemen. "Perhaps the real heroes of the day were the stellar components of the offensive line, Gerry McGowan, Ted Waite, Nick Vrhovac, Bill Bobbora, Gary Winrow, and Dave Doda, who repeatedly opened gaping holes in the Clemson defensive line. Their inside trapping provided unobstructed paths for long jaunts by Larry Hopkins, Larry Russell, Ken Garrett, and Gary Johnson. It seemed the only person in the stadium capable of stopping Hopkins was Coach Stoll himself, who pulled the offensive starters from the game after it became clear we had things well under control for our third consecutive win. Hopkins had done enough damage. The entire team had done enough damage." With the game in hand, Stoll was no doubt preserving players' health for the upcoming battle with North Carolina.

After the final whistle, a reporter found the unassuming Larry Hopkins sitting quietly in front of his locker, oblivious to the fact he had just set an ACC rushing record. That was Hoppy's demeanor—calmly confident, but never boastful or self-congratulatory.

What Hopkins said to the reporter captured the essence of our 1970 team and explained why, more than fifty years later, what we did still resonates. There were no oversized egos. No special treatment for anyone. We played together as a united front. That was what Cal Stoll and his down-ups, color charts, and endless drills had instilled in us.

"I had great blocking at the line of scrimmage," Hopkins told the reporter. "A running back is only as good as his line, and today, our line did the job." Hopkins then did something unusual for a star player. He methodically named each lineman who had made his record-breaking feat possible: Gerald McGowan, Vince Nedimyer, Bill Bobbora, Ted Waite, and Nick Vrhovac—players whose names rarely appeared in newspaper headlines. They were men who had, in many cases, changed positions without complaint when Coach Stoll was assembling his roster during spring practices.

"We beat a good team," Stoll told reporters outside Reynolds Gymnasium. "And that is why I feel so good about the victory. Clemson is a hard-hitting team. It was one of the hardest-hitting games I've been involved in."

He went on to note he would have little time to savor the victory. "Before this game was even over today, I heard the crowd shouting, 'Beat Carolina! Beat Carolina!' I guess we have to forget this Clemson victory and start thinking about North Carolina."

Then, he outlined his grand plan for the remainder of the season. After losing the first three games, he and his coaches had resolved to "even the board." That effort from the coaching staff was what Stoll termed "Phase One." Their strategy for achieving this was abandoning the experimental long ball offense and fully committing to Larry Russell and the veer attack.

Now that the veer offense was humming, Wake Forest was ready to enter Phase Two.

Phase Two was, like Coach Stoll himself, terse and uncomplicated: Beat North Carolina. We would begin Phase Two on Monday morning at practice. We would attempt to complete Phase Two in seven days at Groves Stadium. There was little time or inclination that week for head games. We had a rival to defeat.

The implications of the Clemson game extended beyond the satisfaction of defeating a longtime nemesis. That same afternoon in College Park, Maryland had upset South Carolina 21-15. This unexpected result placed us in a tie for second place in the Atlantic Coast Conference with the University of North Carolina, behind first-place Duke. We were now in a three-way race for the conference championship.

Our win against Clemson proved to be the turning point in our season. But when I look back on it now, I see it not so much as a turning point as a launching pad—for Larry Hopkins. Although Hoppy had shown glimpses of his capabilities in previous games, he exhibited seemingly supernatural powers against the Tigers, leaving fans and players slack-jawed in amazement. It's not often you get to know an athlete with that kind of talent, much less play alongside them.

When Dr. Larry Hopkins, by then a respected Winston-Salem physician and Wake Forest University Trustee, passed away in November 2020 at the age of 70, many of our teammates gathered in Winston-Salem for his memorial service. There, I shared a story with his wife Beth, wishing to somehow convey why Larry meant so much to me, and why so many of his teammates had returned to honor him five decades after we had played together.

I told her my story about one of Larry's breakaway runs in the fourth quarter of that Clemson game, a play that illustrated our teamwork and how we supported each other.

We were backed up on our own 20-yard line. Larry Russell took the snap and moved to his right, reading the defense before handing off to Larry Hopkins, the first man through on the option. Hopkins abruptly cut upfield through the middle, dodging past futilely grabbing, off-balance linemen. Then, as he often did, Hoppy lowered his head and powered past two converging linebackers before cutting to the outside.

He had only one defender left to beat: the safety. That's where I was supposed to intervene. My assignment at tight end called for me to clear out the safety. As the Clemson defender rushed up to make the tackle, all Hopkins could think was, "Where's Dodes? Where's Dodes?"

In a burst of speed fueled by adrenalin, I leaped out in front of Hoppy and flattened the safety. As Hoppy hurdled over both of us, all I could see from my position on the ground was his number 44, moving like lightning upfield. He ran for 50 yards before being tackled on the 21-yard-line. On the next snap he went in for the touchdown.

He knew I'd be there on his 50-yarder. I knew I'd be there too. We never worried about support; it was a given. That was how we played. We had our assignments and we executed them—not for personal glory, but for each other.

I had assumed it was a long-forgotten memory that Beth Hopkins might appreciate hearing. Her response caught me by surprise. "But David," she said, with a knowing smile, "I've heard that story from Larry a hundred times. He told everyone about that play."

That was Larry Hopkins, and that was our team. More than half a century later, we remain that way.

"THE DRIVE"

Our schedule would not get easier after Clemson. The University of North Carolina was up next. Now that we were on a winning path, each successive game became more crucial. We were in the hunt for the ACC crown. If there was a single game we wanted to win, one opponent we were desperate to take down, it was North Carolina. Beating the Tar Heels in a race for the ACC championship would be sublime.

Fueled by decades of competition, the Wake–North Carolina rivalry ran deep. There had been bad blood between the two schools starting with our first matchup in 1888. It was Wake Forest's first-ever football game, and the first collegiate football game played in North Carolina. Wake Forest prevailed 6-4, and UNC had never forgiven us.

We were predicted to lose, but that was nothing new. An upset over the Tar Heels would put us alone in second place in the Atlantic Coast Conference. We set our minds on that task and shut out everything else. Our three-game winning streak—and the surge of confidence that came with it—helped quash any lingering doubts. This was our moment to seize, our chance to prove we belonged.

The oddsmakers, not surprisingly, had made us four-point underdogs despite our three-game winning streak. North Carolina head coach Bill Dooley's Tar Heels ranked fourth in the nation in defense against rushing, our go-to offensive strategy. In six games, they had held opponents to an average of only 76 yards on the ground.

Coach Stoll paid no attention to the numbers. He told reporters he was not inclined to work on our passing game in practice that week nor add anything new to our strategy. "We'll pass if we have to," he said, "but I have a great deal of faith in Larry Russell, Larry Hopkins, Ken Garrett, and Gary Johnson. North Carolina has not been up against a running team like us this year."

Still, there was no question the Tar Heels would be a formidable opponent. Among other standout players, North Carolina was led by hard-running tailback Don McCauley, a future Baltimore Colt who had already amassed 800 yards that season. By the end of the 1970 season, Don would break O. J. Simpson's single-season rushing record of 1,709 yards with 1,720. In addition, Tar Heels' linebacker John Bunting, who went on to play eleven seasons with the Philadelphia Eagles, was an absolute menace on defense.

Larry Lyon of the *Old Gold & Black* pressed Stoll about the challenge we were up against. "We will be facing the strongest team in the conference against the rush this weekend in North Carolina," Stoll acknowledged. "They're real tough, and at the same time our defense will be faced with their biggest challenge," he said, referring to North Carolina's rushing attack led by Don McCauley. "It should be a great game, as both teams are similar offensively and defensively," Stoll added.

In a show of spirited resolve, team leader Win Headley went public for the first time about our players-only meeting after the Florida State loss. He told reporters we had become a "winning team" because of that candid talk among teammates. Win's announcement was either a crafty head game intended to intimidate Tar Heel players—who would read the newspaper accounts of his comments—or a blunder that would motivate them even more to end our streak. Saturday would reveal which.

"We felt we had blown that game with Florida State, and we wanted to know why," Headley explained to reporters. "We set goals, and we fused together. After that, the same old Wake Forest team that wasn't going to beat anybody suddenly won three games in a row. Now we have momentum."

Win elaborated on the metamorphosis of our team culture: "Before Coach Stoll came, we practiced, and during the season, we played together during spring practice and the season. But we weren't close. We only got to know the other defensive players or other offensive players, depending on which unit we played. When the season ended, or spring practice ended, we went our separate ways."

He then explained how things had changed under the new regime. "Coach Stoll organized winter workouts with attendance required. We got to know each other better. We are closer now than we ever were, and right before our toughest game of the season."

As we prepared for the Carolina game, however, complications arose. Our veer offense and its growing effectiveness were no longer a secret. We'd lost the element of surprise. Carolina and its aggressive defense would be well prepared for our standard approach.

While Stoll did not work on extra passing plays to relieve the pressure Larry Russell was sure to face, he did throw in a crucial tactical twist to the veer. We had beaten Clemson by counter-blocking at the line of scrimmage. Stoll and his coaches expanded on that with something they hoped would work well against a tuned-in Carolina—a counter-veer that would, if it worked, flummox the defense, who would likely be mirroring Russell's movement down the line as he weighed his options.

Stoll's "misdirection" strategy was pure genius. If Russell faked left, he would be followed by our backs to draw in the linebackers, as we usually did. But a microsecond later, Russell and the back would move right, freezing the attackers and creating a hole. If our blocking was perfect, we could use the defense's own inertia against them, at least, that was the theory. But beyond offensive strategizing, we faced another challenge. Center Nick Vrhovac, who'd had an outstanding game against Clemson, underwent an emergency appendectomy Tuesday afternoon and was out of action indefinitely—a devastating blow to our offensive line. In his place, Gary German, our 6-foot 4-inch, 210-pound backup center, would step into the breach.

There was barely enough room for spectators to breathe in a packed Groves Stadium on October 24 as we stretched before our biggest game of the season. A record crowd of more than 30,500 fans pressed shoulder-to-shoulder for our much-anticipated collision with favored North Carolina.

From the opening kickoff, both sides adopted a take-no-prisoners attitude. The game developed into a "banger"—a hard-hitting, bruising struggle with low offensive production. Both teams seemed to prefer a sledgehammer approach to moving the ball.

One spectator, a Marine, told a reporter that both teams looked "as if they were trying to plant the flag on Iwo Jima on every play." The comparison was apt. This was combat in cleats, a war in which every yard gained exacted a cost.

Carolina drew first blood. In the first quarter, quarterback Paul Miller passed the Tar Heels down the field, capping the drive with a 4-yard touchdown by McCauley. Tim Craven kicked the extra point for a 7-0 lead. With a few exceptions, our modified counter-veer was ineffective against a strong Tar Heels' defense. We appeared to be thoroughly outmatched.

Though unable to put points on the board, we managed to hold Carolina from adding to their lead until the third quarter, when a 25-yard Miller pass to tight end Tony Blanchard, later drafted by the NFL's Cleveland Browns, put the Tigers at the Deacon 27-yard line. Miller then fired another pass to Blanchard, who caught the ball on the 15-yard line and ran over two defenders into the end zone. Incredulously, Craven missed the extra point, his first misfire in seventeen attempts that season.

We were down 13-0 in the fourth, our offense seemingly unable to get out of second gear. We moved the ball at times, but were unable to maintain a steady drive, let alone score. The game clock continued to wind down on what appeared to be another Wake Forest disappointment.

Late in the third quarter, the counter-veer finally began to reap benefits. Charged with blocking All-America linebacker John Bunting—a devastatingly effective Tar Heel tackler that season—I followed him as he moved with Russell. When Russell counter-veered, Bunting's momentum carried him in the same direction as my block, which made my job much easier. I never once collided head-on with the 6-foot, 1-inch, 220-pound linebacker, because Russ's feints and our misdirection sent him charging the wrong way. Bunting outweighed me by twenty pounds, but each time we made contact, I rolled him to the turf, putting him out of the play at least a dozen times.

On a 16-play, 67-yard march, Russell led us downfield to paydirt. The drive was highlighted by two crucial first down-saving runs by Gary Johnson before Russ sneaked over the goal line. Lounsbury added the extra point.

Trailing by six, we felt a shift. Suddenly there was life on the Wake Forest sideline and in the stands. Hope had replaced resignation among the Demon Deacon faithful.

On the Tar Heels' next possession, our defense forced a fourth-down punt, and Junior Moore called for a fair catch. With three minutes remaining, we had the ball back on our own 8-yard line.

The ninety-two yards between us and the opposing end zone was a non-issue for my teammates and me. A touchdown and an extra point would give us the win. We had a job to finish, and we had time enough to do it.

Nothing was frantic; nothing was rushed. Each player was fully cognizant of what this drive meant and his role in it, whether to make a catch, execute a block, complete a pass, or gain yards on a run. Each man knew with a preternatural certainty that we would accomplish what we needed to. We just had to trust each other.

Any athlete who has competed in any sport can tell you about this rare, transcendent feeling. It might happen only once in a career. Sometimes referred to as a "flow" experience, it's not something one can practice for or fabricate on demand. It just *is*.

After Junior Moore calmly fielded the punt, we went to work. Gary German cleared defenders with textbook blocks. Larry Hopkins ran like a house afire. Larry Russell managed the counter-option with surgical precision. Gary Winrow and Gary Johnson made crucial catches with defenders draped all over them. Tracy Lounsbury prepared himself mentally for what was undoubtedly the most important kick of his life.

No one, not a single player on the field made a mistake that wasn't immediately rectified by a teammate. At each critical juncture, as we methodically ground our way toward the Tar Heel goal line, someone rose to the occasion. Each player called upon to act did what was asked of him—because not doing so meant the end of the game and, effectively, the end of our dream.

Everything aligned perfectly. Hours of practice, the harshness of Cal Stoll's winter program, the mental agony of previous defeats, the accumulated aches, sprains, and contusions—even the dismissive preseason articles—had somehow produced a perfect symmetry, if only for those three glorious minutes.

In my memory, those 180 seconds seem to pass in slow motion...

On the first play from our own 8-yard line, Russell drops back and is sacked for a 2-yard loss. Second down nets neither a gain nor a loss. Facing third down and twelve from the six, Russell connects on a 13-yard pass to Steve Bowden for a desperately needed first down. Exactly two minutes remain.

On first and ten from our 19-yard line, Larry Hopkins explodes through the defense, racing 39 yards to the Tar Heels' 38-yard line. Only a last-ditch tackle by Bunting prevents him from going all the way. One minute and forty seconds shows on the clock.

On the next play, Hoppy is immediately brought to the turf, a reminder that Carolina has no intentions of backing down. Russ, composed as always, completes two consecutive 11-yard passes, the first to Gary Winrow and the second to Gary Johnson. Johnson's catch brings us to the Tar Heels' 7-yard line with fifty-eight seconds remaining.

First and goal. A quick handoff to Hopkins gains two more yards, bringing the ball to the five.

The clock continues to run. Dropping back to pass, our usually dexterous quarterback drops the ball and then awkwardly dribbles it across the turf with his feet in a desperate attempt to regain possession. With three Tar Heel defensemen bearing down on him, he somehow manages to scoop up the pigskin and hang onto it, turning almost certain disaster into a two-yard gain.

Nineteen seconds remain. We are three yards from the end zone. Everyone in the stadium knows what's coming next. Russ hands off to Hoppy, again.

Hopkins cuts right as blockers, led by Gary German, our stand-in center, clear the way. At the goal line, Hoppy is stood up straight by a barricade of Carolina blue. He remains that way for one heart-stopping second. Then, not to be denied, he lowers his head, musters one final surge, and plows through a wall of Tar Heel bodies into the end zone.

By the grace of North Carolina's missed extra point in the first quarter, we are tied at thirteen. With fingers crossed, the home crowd watches in rapture as Tracy Lounsbury boots the ball through the uprights, putting us up by one with only seconds to go.

Our special teams' unit kicks off, eating up a few more seconds. Then our defense takes the field one last time. When Ed Stetz intercepts Paul Miller's desperate Hail Mary pass with no time left, the stadium erupts *in what can only be described as pandemonium: helmets flying into the air, fans pouring out of the stands, my teammates leaping up and down in ecstasy, coaches wildly hugging each other.*

Wake Forest supporters left Groves that afternoon shaking their heads, wondering if what they'd witnessed had actually happened. "It's one of the biggest wins I've ever been involved in," a stunned Cal Stoll told reporters afterward. "It's quite naturally the very biggest one since I've been at Wake Forest." Then he added, "It was a great day for our football squad, our student body, and for Deacon fans everywhere."

Then came the tears—of exhaustion, relief, and redemption. To a man, the entire team was overwhelmed emotionally by what they had experienced: four quarters of epic combat, climaxing in what is still known today as "The Drive," arguably one of the greatest clutch performances in ACC history.

ONE STEP CLOSER

As our team joyfully exited the field, Larry Russell walked slightly ahead of us, lost in his own thoughts. Over and over, he tossed his helmet in the air, catching it by the facemask and then slapping it. Coming as it did at the end of three extremely stress-filled weeks, this post-victory ritual offered a welcome release.

A few minutes earlier, exuberant Wake Forest fans had rushed onto the field in a wave of black and gold before following us out of the stadium. Like an incoming tide, dozens of supporters surrounded Russ, slapping him on the back, shouting praise, and trying to hug him. Two excited fans grabbed Russ's left hand and thrust it in the air in a universal sign of victory.

More fans joined the procession, and as the crowd pressed closer, it looked like things were about to spin out of control. Suddenly, Russ appeared to be in more danger of being hurt than he'd been while facing down Carolina's defensive line.

Stoll hurried to catch up, hoping to prevent his starting quarterback from being crushed or carried off on someone's unsteady shoulders. Seething, he pushed and shoved his way through the sea of bodies until he faced the throbbing mob. Spreading his arms wide, he yelled at the team. "Get inside. Now!" Even amid the jubilation, the urgency in his voice was unmistakable. The crowd quickly dispersed, and we retreated to the safety of our locker room.

Once we were downstairs, Stoll gently pulled Russell aside and guided him back up to meet the large group of reporters waiting to hear his reactions. "I'll let Larry speak to you briefly," he told the throng equipped with notepads and recorders, "but I want him to go back with the team to campus and celebrate."

In front of the press, Russ spoke with raw emotion. He would have more to say later but chose to share what he was thinking as he entered the game for that final drive.

"Three weeks ago today, I lost someone very close to me," he said, his eyes welling up with tears. "When something like that happens, it draws you closer to the most important things in your life. I prayed and asked Him to let me do my job on the field."

Then he turned and hurried down to be with his teammates and bask in the splendor of that memorable afternoon. We showered, grabbed our bags, and hopped on the bus for the short ride back to campus.

After Russell departed from the press conference at Groves, Stoll told reporters the win had produced "the biggest game of my life." As he scanned the small room, crammed with media standing shoulder to shoulder, his stern expression softened. A year before, he would have been explaining why we had lost another game. His task on this day was exponentially more palatable.

"I've been involved in a lot of games as an assistant coach at Michigan State," he continued. "And since I've been here, the victory over North Carolina State in my first game here last year was a good one. But this is the best. I have the finest assistant coaches in America, and I could sit here all day and talk about my team."

Before joining us on the buses back to campus, Stoll summarized his thoughts to the press. "A little bit of me dies every time we lose," Stoll said. "I lie awake at night trying to think of ways to psych the team up, ways to get them aroused. They'll never play as well as I want them to. No coach will ever have a perfect team, but I can get them to play as well as they can."

Stoll paused. But for the hiss of tape recorders, you could have heard a pin drop. "We're not winning because we have an abundance of talent. Winning is about attitude. Properly stimulated, lesser teams will outperform more talented teams. It is my job to stimulate."

Then, the stoic coach broke character, finally giving voice to his true feelings. "I think we are at the point that I can say we have a pretty good football team." For him, it was as close to bragging as he had ever come.

When we emerged from Reynolds Gym, an astonishing sight awaited us. The center of campus was completely transformed. Every tree along the entire length and breadth of Hearn Plaza—known colloquially as "The Quad"—was covered in an avalanche of toilet paper. In front of Wait Chapel, white tissue streamers ran twenty and thirty feet down from the elms, dogwoods, willow oaks, and magnolias towering above The Quad's walkways. Covered by windblown tissue, the scene resembled a Hallmark Christmas card—a winter wonderland in October.

How this came about in less than an hour—never mind how students had managed to scrounge enough toilet paper to create what looked like the aftermath of a sudden blizzard—remains a mystery to me. But it was beautiful—a dazzling white celebration for an accomplishment that had been years in the making. Wake Forest football as we knew it was transformed. The impossible had suddenly become possible.

Almost immediately, the *Old Gold and Black* announced it would devote an entire issue to the game. The significance wasn't lost on any of us; this was history in the making, worthy of documentation.

In his article titled, "An Unassuming Hero," Charlie Dayton wrote: "The scoreboard clock shows 19 seconds remaining. Wake has no timeouts left, and the ball is on the Carolina 3-yard line. Quarterback Larry Russell takes the snap and hands it off to Larry Hopkins, who is apparently stopped at the one. But with Herculean second and third efforts, 'Hoppy' pushes his way into the end zone to set off the wildest victory celebration seen in years at the usually placid Baptist school. Only a week before, the quiet and unassuming Hopkins had thrust himself into the spotlight by establishing a new ACC rushing record of 230 yards. Despite his recent achievements, Hopkins finds it difficult to adjust to his newfound popularity. The hero role does not fit the shy, polite chemistry major who seems much more at ease studying in Z. Smith Reynolds Library than answering the probing questions of inquisitive sports writers."

Those words captured something essential about our team—we were not natural-born stars or glory seekers. We were students and athletes—a bunch of ordinary young men who found ourselves at the epicenter of a thrilling sports narrative.

DOWN BUT
NOT OUT

The following game was in Memphis, a non-conference match against ninth-ranked Tennessee. After the Volunteers, we would face our last two ACC rivals, Duke and North Carolina State. "We've got to keep momentum on our side," Stoll warned. "The damn bubble can break so easily."

On Monday, we descended from the clouds we'd been walking on since Saturday. As soon as we hit the practice field, the abysmal state of our physical condition became agonizingly clear.

It was inevitable. Hard-fought wins exact a price. We had beaten the odds three weeks in a row, defied our detractors, and made staunch believers out of our ambivalent fans. The North Carolina game, a victory as fulfilling as any of us had ever experienced, had drained us physically and emotionally.

My teammates and I paid dearly for our hard-hitting style, which, when paired with a lack of depth, left little time on the bench for a breather. Our ranks were thinning, and our trainer, Doc, was busier than ever.

Gary Johnson had torn knee ligaments and needed surgery to repair them. He was gone for the season. Nick Vrhovac was recovering from his appendectomy. Win Headley was on crutches. Meanwhile, the rest of us tried to imperson- ate healthy players, hiding winces and limps, knowing that to show weakness was to invite doubt in ourselves or, worse, in each other. One player stood out in the best actor category, embodying everything Stoll had been trying to instill in us from day one.

Archie Logan had gone into the North Carolina game nursing sore ribs, not the best condition for a defensive lineman who would take hits on every play. Though Archie kept it to himself, he tore ligaments in his left knee in the first quarter. The pain had to have been unbearable, yet he pushed through it, staying in the game to the final whistle.

Informed Sunday about Archie's heroics, Stoll told Mary Garber, "That shows what he's made of." Coming from a coach whose primary objective was to exact the absolute maximum from us, that simple statement constituted high praise.

We had four more games, two of which would decide the ACC champi- onship. No one talked about it, but we resolved to show Stoll we were just as tough as Archie. His stoicism while enduring unimaginable pain became our benchmark, a standard by which we measured our own commitment.

The *Old Gold & Black* set the stage for what we faced against Tennessee. "The Big Orange enter the game with a 5-1 record, having suffered its only loss to Auburn, 36-23. The Vols have won handily over SMU (28-3), Army (48-3), Georgia Tech (17-6), Alabama (24-0), and Florida (38-7)."

Our game would be the seventh confrontation between Wake Forest and Tennessee, each team having won three games in a history dating back to 1892. The scheduling gods had shown no mercy, pitting us against a fast, aggressive Volunteers team set on strutting its potent offense for the national pollsters.

Coach Stoll didn't mince words about our impending opponent, telling the press corps, "Tennessee has one of the finest teams in the country. They have the best passing attack we've faced this season. They are strong in every phase of the game, which is why they rank among the best. It's a tremendous challenge for our team."

The game can be described in five plays that still haunt me.

First, Tennessee scored after a bad first-half center snap to punter Tracy Lounsbury deep in our territory. As Tennessee defenders swarmed him, Tracy never had a chance, the football bouncing awkwardly before being recovered by the Volunteers.

Second, we put together a promising drive late in the third quarter that brought us all the way to the Vols' 4-yard line before Larry Hopkins dove into the end zone for the score. Our bench ignited in celebration, but the play was called back on an illegal motion penalty, and we entered the fourth quarter with nothing to show for our efforts.

Third, Larry Russell missed a wide-open Steve Bowden on a quick, short pass to the end zone, a routine connection we'd completed countless times in practice.

Fourth, Lounsbury had an easy field goal blocked.

And finally, Russell missed me on a pass from the Tennessee 27-yard line—a play on which I felt sure I would have scored. I remember the heartache of watching that ball sail just beyond my outstretched fingers, taking with it our last real opportunity.

Except for a 61-yard touchdown in the first half by Junior Moore, our offense was unable to score. Larry Lyon covered the game succinctly in the *Old Gold & Black*. "Tennessee had little trouble in handling the out-manned Deacons, who appeared flat after their emotional victory over North Carolina the week before. The Volunteers led 27-7 at halftime and coasted the rest of the way with reserves. The loss snapped Wake's four-game win string, the longest compiled by a Deacon team since 1967 when they won four in a row at the close of the season. One must go back to 1944 before a five-game streak is found, which will have to wait until next year now."

Led by future NFL quarterback Bobby Scott and boasting fifteen players who could run the forty in under 4.6 seconds, Tennessee was a juggernaut we were not prepared to meet after the draining North Carolina win. Our banged-up defense, still nursing wounds from previous battles, could not keep pace with their speed and precision. Final score: 41-7 in favor of the Volunteers.

Tennessee finished the 1970 season ranked fourth nationally after a Sugar Bowl win over Air Force. In retrospect, we had faced one of the nation's elite teams when at our most vulnerable.

It was one of those days—fortunately, a rare day. Even more fortunately, our one-sided loss to a non-conference team was irrelevant. We remained in second place at 3-1 in the ACC behind 4-0 Duke. Scheduled to meet the Blue Devils the following Saturday in Durham, we had one week to get back on track. Our locker room after the Tennessee game was quiet, but not despondent.

God bless Mary Garber and her agile writing. A connoisseur of subjective reporting, she came as close as she could to offering an apology for our efforts against Tennessee in her post-game account, drawing attention to our effort rather than our demoralizing loss.

"Those who are close to the Wake Forest football team know their wins came from hustle and heart as much as ability. The Deacons have played well and are dedicated young men who performed, in some cases, better than they really are. Not that the Deacons are an overrated football team whose balloon deserved to be punctured. The Deacs have worked hard, and they believe they have become a sound football team. They are still."

Her words soothed the sting of defeat, reminding us, and our fans, that one loss defined neither our season nor our character.

Stoll admitted we were spent before the Tennessee game. Talking with reporters afterward, he said, "We were flat today, but I thought their defense had something to do with it. They do not have a weakness. We were drained emotionally after last week's game and had played well for the last four weeks."

Despite the loss, Stoll remained optimistic. He brushed it off, and we returned to practice Monday, ready for our next biggest game of the season in what had become a season of next biggest games.

Duke had beaten Virginia, North Carolina State, Clemson, and Maryland. In their non-conference matchups against the bigger schools, they had performed admirably, losing 34-10 to number one Ohio State and 21-19 to Florida.

Offensive coordinator Oval Jaynes summed up our situation with characteristic frankness. "We had a mental letdown and were inconsistent against Tennessee," he told reporters. "We can't afford to do that against Duke." Then, he specified what we needed to do to win. "We must be more consistent and are going to have to take advantage of our scoring opportunities, something we did not do against Tennessee." Jaynes understood the challenge facing us. "Their defensive unit has given up very few points. Other than Ohio State, who scored 34 points, and Florida, who scored 21, no opponent has scored more than 12 points against them."

We had seven days. Seven days to heal our bodies, restore our confidence, and reignite our passion. The Tennessee game was behind us. Duke and our conference championship dreams lay ahead.

SHOWDOWN
IN DURHAM

Two weeks ago, everyone was hailing the Wake-Carolina game as the biggest game for Wake Forest in many years," wrote Larry Lyon in the *Old Gold & Black*. "It was, and the Deacs came through to win. But forget all that now. Now it's the ACC championship up for grabs. Wake Forest at Duke at Wallace Wade Stadium in Durham. If Wake wins, they will take a giant step toward their first ACC championship ever, and if they should lose, they will be eliminated from contention. Duke's Blue Devils are perched in first place in the conference standings with a perfect 4-0 record. Wake follows with their 3-1 mark."

As we inched our way into contention, several North Carolina sportswriters referred to our quest as "the impossible dream." Beating Duke, whom we had succumbed to 20-27 on our home turf in 1969, was essential. If we lost in Durham, the dream, impossible or not, would be over.

The ultra-cautious Cal Stoll touched briefly on something he rarely mentioned—winning the conference. "We've got a shot at it now," he told the members of the Sportsman's Club at their weekly luncheon meeting before the

Tennessee game. "But I'd like to get through the conference schedule before I get on Cloud Nine."

There was no denying the facts stacked against us: We had beaten Duke only once since 1951; they had future NFL quarterback Leo Hart; they were undefeated in the Atlantic Coast Conference; and their colossal defensive line had spent all week preparing to stop Larry Russell and our veer offense. But the facts didn't scare us. We couldn't have cared less. As we prepared for our showdown with the Blue Devils, we held tight to an unwavering belief in ourselves.

The eight-mile drive to Durham on game day felt like a victory parade waiting to happen. As we dressed in the locker room, there were none of the usual pregame jitters. We stretched before kickoff surrounded by 28,600 fans, many of them ours—a benefit of playing an away game so close to home.

We believed in ourselves. This was our game to win. Duke was nothing more than an obstacle in our path—a speed bump on the road to what we wanted.

From the opening kickoff, we were revved up and raring to go. On his first carry of the day, Larry Russell broke free for 29 yards. His first rush, one reporter noted, "should have been a warning that Wake Forest came to play football."

In the first quarter, our offense rolled 54 yards—twenty-one of them on a pass to Gary Winrow—before Russ ran it in from the six. Duke took the kickoff and moved from its 29 to our 13, but Hart fumbled, and John "BJ" Phillips recovered on the Wake 24.

In the second quarter, we doubled our lead to 14-0 on a 56-yard touchdown drive that culminated in Ken Garrett going over from the three.

In the third quarter, we staged another 56-yard drive, extending our lead to 21-0. Russell scored again, this time going over from the eight.

Then Coach Stoll made an unprecedented move: He pulled many of the starters. This wasn't due to overconfidence or a show of altruism to avoid embarrassing Duke Head Coach Tom Harp. The lead wasn't insurmountable, but thus far, we had controlled every aspect of the game.

None of the juniors or seniors who had played under Stoll had ever witnessed such a wholesale substitution with more than a quarter left to play. Then again, none of us had ever played in a game where we were so clearly in command.

Stoll was already thinking ahead to North Carolina State the following week. Eight games into the season, we were beaten up. Walking over to the bench, we peeled tape from our fingers and wrists, removed our helmets, and sat down. It was an unexpected relief to be spectators for the first time that year, or even the past two years.

Our respite, sadly, was short-lived. Quarterback Leo Hart immediately went to work against our second-string defense. Late in the third, after moving the ball 64 yards in 11 plays, Hart dove in from the two. On Duke's first possession in the fourth, he scored again from the three to climax an 81-yard march.

Suddenly, injuries, rest for NC State, and our well-deserved break lost their relevance. The upcoming game would be meaningless if we didn't finish off Duke.

We strapped on our helmets and scrambled back into the game. Not long after, Russell orchestrated an impressive 80-yard, 13-play drive for our fourth score, courtesy of a 30-yard pass to Gary Winrow followed by Ken Garrett's nine-yard sprint into the end zone for the TD. It was Ken's best game yet, rushing for 141 yards on 23 carries, including two touchdowns.

Duke had no answer for Garrett that afternoon. According to the *Old Gold & Black,* "Throughout the 1970 season, coach Cal Stoll insisted that Ken Garrett was a back with exceptional talents. The flashy junior college transfer raced over, around, and through baffled Duke defenders as Wake Forest's incredible Deacons overwhelmed the Blue Devils. Other members of the Deacon squad were also quite impressive as the preseason conference doormats continued their Cinderella journey through the 1970s schedule."

By the final whistle, Duke had lost six starters to injury, including Hart, all of whom watched helplessly from the sideline as our team, the team everyone had picked to finish last, ended the game tied for first in the ACC.

Larry Russell was the game MVP, executing the veer offense with the precision of a master violinist playing a finely tuned Stradivarius. One reporter described our star QB as "a magician, running the option magnificently." Russ finished the afternoon with 108 yards rushing, while his sleight of hand unleashed Larry Hopkins for 106 more up the middle. But while Russell and Hopkins surprised no one, including Duke's defense, it was Ken Garrett's day to shine. Finally healthy after nursing a bad ankle all season, Ken had his best performance yet, rushing for 141 yards and two touchdowns.

But we didn't only gain yards on the ground. To keep the Blue Devils guessing, Russell took to the air eight times, completing five passes for 73 yards, including a one-handed catch by Steve Bowden coming out of the backfield.

We won 28-14, but the score doesn't reflect our total domination. The Blue Devils were in Wake territory only twice in the first half. We ran 44 plays in the first half compared to only 26 for Duke. We finished with 352 yards rushing. More importantly, we controlled the clock by running 86 total offensive plays. Duke's offense had little opportunity to do anything but watch our show from the sideline. It was Cal Stoll football: ball-control to perfection.

As the seconds ticked down, our fans began to chant, "We're number one! We're number one!" Before time expired, Russ sealed the deal with a simple quarterback sneak.

Our entire team rushed onto the field, shouting and leaping, slapping and pounding each other, and embracing anyone within reach. The Wake Forest Band struck up a raucous version of "Here's to Wake Forest," our faithful fans loudly singing along. As we headed to the visitors' locker room, Russ had the game ball tucked securely under his arm.

A group of supporters immediately surrounded Cal Stoll, as respected journalist Mary Garber approached him. "We did it," he said. Three words that encapsulated nearly two years of hard work, disappointment, and frustration. "I can't imagine more of a team victory than we had today," he told Garber.

Mary captured the moment in her inimitable style. "Russell was magnificent. As always, there was reliable Larry Hopkins, who churned up yardage and defensive backs in his usual 106 yards to give him a total of 853 for the season. Steve Bowden, the often-forgotten man with Wake Forest's crushing ground attack, made two circus catches in front of the stunned Duke crowd. Gary Winrow had a big catch. Win Headley, Eddie Stetz, Frank Fussell, Terry Kuharchek, all of the defense played well. They did what they had to do."

The fans continued their "We're number one!" chant as they surrounded Stoll on his way to the locker room. Stoll turned to the most exuberant supporter and cautioned, "You're a little premature. We have to beat State, and Duke has to lose again for the number one to become permanent."

That Sunday, The Winston-Salem Journal published an opinion piece that typically would have been reserved for the editorial page or political section. It carried no byline, but we all recognized it as the work of our most loyal advocate, Mary Garber.

It was a heartfelt plea for fans to show up in force for the North Carolina State game. "For anybody who loves never-say-die football, the Demon Deacons of 1970 are a fascinating bunch to watch. This year, the Wake Forest team has been opening some eyes for good reasons. It has more confidence in itself than it has speed. It is superbly drilled, and all those things are difficult for laymen to assess. We suspect that Coach Stoll and his assistants like and admire their boys as people, not merely as football players, and that the attitude is reciprocated. It is riding so high just now that it is ripe for a thumping upset by North Carolina State at Groves Stadium Saturday. That is the common expectation among many football experts at any rate, but Cal Stoll's Deacons are an uncommon team, and any football fan who misses the last chance to see them play at home this year will surely regret it."

The *Raleigh News & Observer* revived the familiar refrain about Wake Forest football. "The North Carolina State game now appears to be a much bigger task for Wake Forest. There is no question about State's going to Winston ready for an all-out effort to avenge the last-second 22-21 defeat pinned on the Wolfpack last season in its opener with Wake Forest."

With a genuine ACC Championship within reach, media coverage of our bid for the championship exploded. Charlie Dayton wrote a special tribute to "Unsung Heroes" in the *Old Gold & Black*. "The scene is a familiar one, Larry Russell takes the step and hands off to fullback Larry Hopkins. Or Russell may elect to keep the ball and slip between pursuing defenders. Sometimes, Larry decides to take a third option and pitches back to fleet Kenny Garrett. Regardless of which alternative Russell chooses, the result is usually the same, a gain of four, maybe five, yards... But unfortunately, there is one group of men who are often overlooked in the flowing accolades. These are the faceless heroes of the offensive linemen, such as Vince Nedimyer, Gerry McGowan, Nick Vrhovac, Gary German, Ted Waite, Tom Martin, Bill Bobbora, Gary Winrow, and Dave Doda.

"Theirs is not a job of glory, but if they do not perform well, no records are broken. There are no wins over Carolina and Duke. There is no chance for an ACC championship. Obviously, the Wake Forest offensive line has done their job exceptionally well."

As the new week dawned and the magnitude of our opportunity crystallized before us, we felt the unmistakable pull of destiny. We were forged to win—not to share a title or settle for honorable mention, but to claim the championship outright. The path to the conference championship was clear: Duke would face the formidable challenges of South Carolina and North Carolina, while we would be battling North Carolina State on our home turf the following week. Everything was there for us to seize the moment and etch our names in history as the undisputed 1970 ACC Champions.

THE IMPOSSIBLE DREAM

When we showed up for Monday's practice, we noticed Cal Stoll had reached deep inside his bag of motivational tools. Our practice field, not far from The Quad and across from Babcock Hall, a women's dorm, was surrounded by a temporary fence that blocked anyone from seeing what was going on inside. More to the point, it blocked us from looking at the scenery when Cal Stoll and his coaches wanted us to be paying attention.

It was no secret we enjoyed that location. It put us at center stage and offered the opportunity—on the rare occasions when our coaches weren't looking—for players to enjoy the attentions of any female students who might happen to walk by. The North Carolina State game called for our undivided attention; Stoll shut it down.

"That's a great big open space out there," Stoll told surprised reporters who came by Monday afternoon. "It's not conducive to practice. There are coeds walking by and other distracting things. It's disturbing. We want complete concentration."

181

Every day that week, Stoll employed a new method of motivation. He was psyching us up for the biggest game of our lives. And it worked—a little too well. After our final pregame practice Friday afternoon, we were so pumped to destroy our rivals we didn't want to wait until Saturday. Before heading to the showers, a few players began to shout that they wanted to play immediately. More joined in, and soon the entire team was yelling in unison, hopping up and down, calling for the game to start. Our excitement reached the point where Stoll felt the need to intervene. He calmly stepped in and told us to take deep breaths and relax.

He was right and we knew it. North Carolina State was dead set on ending our quest for the ACC title. We needed a night of rest before the biggest game of our lives. Tomorrow would come soon enough.

Our final Atlantic Coast Conference game against North Carolina State was more than an important game: It meant everything—to both teams. Still angry and embarrassed over 1969's last-minute loss to us in front of their home crowd, the Wolfpack was hungry for revenge. For us, it meant the culmination of our season and, for many, the last ACC game of our football careers. The implications were paramount: Lose, and our chance for a first-place finish was over. Win, and we had a solid shot at being crowned ACC champions.

As compelling an athletic contest as the game was touted to be, from a fan perspective, it was underwhelming for three reasons. First, there was the weather. Spectators shivered under umbrellas as rain drizzled down most of the afternoon. Second, perhaps due in part to the weather, the game turned out to be a defensive battle, with neither offense scoring a touchdown until the fourth quarter. And, finally, there was the waiting and hoping for some sign that one's favorite team was about to take charge.

It was a long wait.

In the first half, our finely tuned veer was ineffective, forcing our offense to switch to the seldom-used passing game. Furthermore, our ball-control offense had very little control and, often, no ball. We only crossed over into Wolfpack territory once, in the final minutes of the second quarter: Two short passes by Larry Russell and a 38-yard aerial from halfback Junior Moore to Steve Bowden enabled Wake to move to the State 15. Tracy Lounsbury kicked a field goal from twenty-two yards out to knot the score at 3-3.

In the third quarter, the Wolfpack continued to dominate as they had in the first half. Our offense had possession for less than two minutes total. My offensive teammates and I watched glumly from the sidelines as our defense battled to keep us in the game. Larry Russell spent so little time on the field that he ran and threw passes on the sideline to stay warm.

Thankfully, our defense, led by Eddie Stetz, kept us alive, allowing State only two field goals in three quarters of play. Pound-for-pound one of the most prolific tacklers in the ACC, Eddie was a one-man wrecking crew, making sixteen tackles and assisting on eleven others.

Two plays in particular earned the junior classman from Johnstown, Pennsylvania, National "Lineman of the Week" accolades from the Associated Press. Up 6-3 in the third quarter, NC State's offense was backed up to its own 25-yard-line on fourth down. The Wolfpack sent in their special teams, and, on the next play, as the ball flew off the foot of State punter Allen Hicks, Eddie busted through the line and blocked it, sending it bouncing into their end zone. Pat McHenry pounced on it for a touchdown. A successful PAT by Lounsbury put us in the lead 10-6.

Our opponents did not let up. On the ensuing kickoff, State's Pat Kenney ripped off a 50-yard return followed by a successful drive by quarterback Dennis Britt, bringing NC State to fourth and goal at the one-foot line. In a goal-line stand that brought the capacity crowd to its feet, Stetz and Headley stuffed Dave Rodgers' attempted fullback dive. The score stood at 10-6.

On our next possession, Russell was unable to put together a drive. Our defense returned to the field, exhausted. Britt threw a touchdown pass to Kenney that put the Wolfpack up 13-10 with 13 minutes still to play in the fourth quarter.

With just over six minutes to go, our offense finally came alive. Russ, with the help of Hopkins, led the team downfield on a sustained drive that brought us to the Wolfpack 10-yard line. We lined up for the snap, poised and ready to do some damage.

On first down, Russ began an option play to the left, looking for Larry Hopkins, but the Wolfpack defense trapped him with nowhere to go. A split second before he would have been smothered for a loss, Russ, his arms pinned, somehow managed to shove a chest pass to Ken Garrett on the 6-yard line. Ken grabbed it and, with a Wolfpack defender hanging on his back, turned and dove into the end zone. It wasn't the prettiest completion ever made, but fortunately for Wake, touchdowns aren't graded on beauty. Unfortunately, Tracy

Lounsbury, who had kicked 20 consecutive extra points, missed the first PAT of his Wake Forest career, putting more pressure on a defense that had fought under pressure all afternoon.

We now led 16-13 with two and a half minutes remaining. State returned our kickoff to their own 30-yard line. On the first play, Eddie Stetz hit their rusher hard, causing him to fumble after a 14-yard run. Terry Kuharchek fell on the loose ball at the Wolfpack 44. Determined to use up as much time as possible, we deployed a heavily guarded ground offense for two solid minutes before punting with 27 seconds to go.

In a last-ditch attempt to salvage a game they had controlled from the opening kickoff, North Carolina State's offense continued its assault. And once again, led by Eddie, our defense shut them down in their own end. With only a few precious seconds remaining, NC State was left with one last option: a bomb to the end zone.

On the final play, as time ran out, Britt threw a Hail Mary pass. It was intercepted by Dick Bozoian, who ran upfield until a Wolfpack lineman knocked him out of bounds and into a row of hedges well off the sideline. Dick recalls, "When I crawled out of the bushes, I remember some branches from the bushes sticking out of my helmet. I thought that I would be greeted by my teammates, but they had all rushed to the center of the field and were whooping it up with fans and cheerleaders. I remember standing there alone with the intercepted football."

The stadium was a throng of benevolent bedlam. Several players lifted Cal Stoll to their shoulders and carried him to the center of the field, his right arm extended over his head, index finger in the air. Despite our mistakes, and despite being outplayed most of the game, we had found a way to win—thanks to Ed Stetz and our stalwart defense. We carried Stoll off the field, dancing and leaping beside him, surrounded by hundreds of exuberant fans.

Police cars, their sirens screaming, escorted our buses from Groves Stadium back to Reynolds Gymnasium. As always, the campus was festooned with toilet paper. There, we were met by girlfriends, parents, relatives, and friends with hugs and, of course, tears of joy and relief.

That scene, over 55 years ago, is frozen in time for all of us, something we can return to in a heartbeat. Even now, it remains unfathomable. What we went through, how we never gave up, how we bonded, and how we ultimately prevailed. We lived a dream that few attain. Not only did we pull off a glorious come-from-behind win, but we also gave Wake Forest its first winning season since 1959 and its first "Big-Four" title—a traditional sports rivalry between the "Tobacco Road" schools North Carolina, Duke, Wake Forest, and NC State—since 1951. Most rewarding of all, we now had an actual chance of becoming the Deacons' first-ever Atlantic Coast Conference champions.

We showered, changed, headed home, and turned on the radio broadcast of the Duke–South Carolina game. Eddie Stetz listened while holding the game ball he had been awarded for his outstanding play.

Cal Stoll went home and put on a black baseball cap bearing a large white "1" on its crown, a gift he had received months before from one of his assistants. He told a reporter who had come along that it was the first time he'd worn the hat. "I'm too superstitious," he admitted.

Our effort left us momentarily tied for first place in the ACC with Duke. The Blue Devils—who beat South Carolina later that night 42-28—would decide our fate the following week when they played North Carolina.

It all came down to one game, and we would not be playing in it. A North Carolina win over Duke on November 21 would put us alone in first place. For the first time in Wake Forest history, our team and our supporters would be rooting for the despised Tar Heels.

The *Old Gold & Black* summed up the odd situation: "Since the beginning of the Wake Forest, North Carolina football rivalry 82 years ago, there have been few, if any, times when the Old Gold and Black faithful have been found cheering for their bitter Chapel Hill foe. However, the Duke–Carolina clash will find that unheard-of phenomenon occurring wherever Wake students, alumni, and fans may gather. The reason for this strange switching of allegiances is no secret. A Tar Heel victory or tie at Kenan Stadium will give the incredible Demon Deacons their first football championship ever in a year in which they were a solid preseason pick for the conference cellar."

We had done our part. We had made our own luck, finishing our six-game ACC schedule with a 5-1 record and effectively eliminating the other contenders in the tight race. South Carolina, NC State, Clemson, Maryland, Virginia, and North Carolina, were out. If luck were to intervene next week, we fervently hoped it would land on the side of North Carolina.

In essence, our season was over. The die was cast. Our last game on the schedule was against 19th-ranked Houston, a national powerhouse. As the

Cougars were not in our conference, the game was of no consequence. But in an ironic twist, Houston was coached by Bill Yoeman, the man who, five years earlier, was the first to use the veer offense. Up to now, we had him to thank for the 1970 season's success.

FROM DREAM
TO REALITY

We arrived at the Houston Marriot on Friday. Our game, meanwhile, was scheduled for 7 o'clock Saturday night, which meant we had an entire day to kill. Being stuck in the hotel not knowing the outcome of the Duke–North Carolina game was unbearable. Players couldn't sit still or manage a conversation for more than thirty seconds. There was none of the usual kidding, horseplay, or joking around. Like most of my teammates, I wanted to be left alone in my own nervous state while awaiting the results. Except for an occasional ding from the elevators, the hotel hallways were silent. The suspense was killing us.

Our victories against both the Tar Heels and the Blue Devils had no bearing on determining the conference champion. If Duke prevailed, we would each have one loss, but they would have six conference wins to our five and be crowned champions. If Duke lost, we would each have five conference wins—but they would have two conference losses to our one—and we would be champions.

Stoll had arranged for us to hear the radio broadcast of the pivotal game in a hotel conference room before our team dinner. A few guys took Stoll up on his offer, but most of us were far too antsy to sit and listen, and, therefore, did not know the outcome until he came and told us. Even Stoll did not attend the broadcast he'd arranged, choosing to retreat to his room and watch the Ohio State–Michigan game on TV.

On the other hand, our group of traveling supporters was quite interested in listening to the game. They gathered in the hotel's main ballroom, drinking champagne and celebrating every Tar Heel score. Everyone on the first floor of the Marriott could hear them. Mostly, they were cheering for Carolina's star tail back Don McCauley—whom we had kept in check as best as anyone could keep Don in check. But that afternoon he ran with abandon, scoring five touchdowns against the hapless Blue Devils.

When the game ended and Stoll heard that North Carolina had won, he came downstairs as we gathered for the pregame meal. His announcement took a while to sink in. There were a few cheers, but we did not go wild. If anything, we were dumbstruck. After you have wanted something so badly, worked so hard for it for so long, and been told it was a ridiculous goal to even think about, when it finally does happen it becomes almost incomprehensible.

It is odd now when I think about it. We were exhausted physically from the long season. But we were also worn down emotionally. Living for an entire week with the knowledge that our goal of being conference champions was entirely out of our hands had taken its toll. It did not help that we had to go out the next day and play a top-tier team featuring future Dallas Cowboys superstar fullback Robert Newhouse. We heard Stoll's news, put it on hold, and pretended to care about the Houston game. We wanted to celebrate—God knows we were ready. But we had to tamp down our emotions. We had a game to play.

On Saturday, our minds were elsewhere. The artificial turf of the Astrodome was hard and merciless, much like our opponents. But we had to get past Houston before we could celebrate. It was like being told a much-needed and well-deserved vacation would start right after an emergency root canal. Truth be told, the game was meaningless: Our season had ended the moment Cal Stoll gathered us together before Friday's pregame dinner and announced, "Gentlemen, you are the Atlantic Coast Conference Champions."

We were distracted, and it showed. We had forty-six penalties called against, no doubt some sort of record. The Cougars crushed us 26-2 in a game not one of us was interested in playing.

As we showered and prepared for our charter flight back to Winston-Salem, the enormity of what we had done began to sink in. We had done what everyone said we were incapable of doing. What we accomplished is still sinking in now; that's the incredible beauty of it.

As our bus pulled up in front of Reynolds Gymnasium in the wee hours of Sunday morning, we were met by hundreds of fans who had shrugged off the cold, blocked off the road, and whooped, danced, and sung for two hours in the dark while we made the final leg of the trip.

We watched in awe as supporters surrounded our buses, still chanting as they welcomed us back to campus. It felt like a scene straight out of a movie. The most graceful description of what it felt like to win the Atlantic Conference Championship came fifty-four years later from a supporter who was on the bus and witnessed that predawn scene. Beth Hopkins—then Beth Norbrey and dating Larry Hopkins—had traveled with us to our season finale as a clarinetist with the marching band. Recalling that moment, Beth said, "Larry held my hand, smiled deeply, and was in unusually high spirits as the team, and he, welcomed the heap of praise from the students. It was a glorious night that I will never forget." Every one of us who witnessed that spectacle, even now, would say the same.

For weeks, we were fêted with events honoring our storybook season. The first actually took place on the plane ride home when flight attendants served us a steak dinner. Throughout the two-hour journey, we basked in the praise of our loyal traveling supporters. Celebrations did not end until close to a month later with a barbeque and fried chicken dinner hosted by Wake Forest President James Ralph Scales featuring a gold and black cake that was a miniature replica of Groves Stadium. We ate everything up that month, literally and figuratively.

In between were highlights only a championship team could understand. The on-campus festivities began before kickoff in Houston. At 4:20 Saturday afternoon, following the conclusion of North Carolina's rout of Duke, more than 400 students papered The Quad and shot off strings of fireworks. Students danced to rock music blaring from nearby dorm windows and chugged beer from cans wrapped in paper towels in an impromptu victory festival.

Then came the accolades—and there were many. Cal Stoll was voted Atlantic Conference Coach of the Year, an announcement he accepted on behalf of his assistants. Mary Garber—once again setting aside her journalistic impartiality—could not help but note, "The man behind it all is the one who made the Deacons players believe in themselves and each other, which has been a basic ingredient of Wake Forest's success."

Stoll's tour de force did not go unnoticed in the college football world at large. By the end of the week, he was offered the head coaching job at Florida State, prompting a day of unnerving drama before he turned it down, saying he was committed to Wake Forest. As only Coach Stoll would do, he took advantage of the press conference to announce that practices for the 1971 season would be tougher than those of our championship year.

Deacon players also garnered attention. Six—Bill Bobbora, Win Headley, Larry Hopkins, Larry Russell, Tracy Lounsbury, and Eddie Stetz—were named to the All-ACC team. In addition, Headley—the only senior in the group—was chosen to play in two all-star showcases for NFL scouts, the North-South game in Miami on Christmas Day and the North-South American Bowl in Tampa on January 10.

The most magnificent evening of our welcome-home celebration occurred on December 15 at a season-ending awards banquet in our honor. It was held in Bridger Field House in a big open conference room—lavishly decked out in black and gold—that overlooked Groves Stadium. On the players' tables, each place setting featured a championship watch and ceramic mug commemorating our unprecedented achievement.

The event was emceed by Billy Packer—1962 Wake Forest alumnus, former Deacon basketball star, and future award-winning NCAA Final Four basketball commentator. He opened by reading the words: "No Offense, No Defense, No Hope!" The room broke out in cheers. Billy then followed with a selection of choice headlines and clippings predicting our last-place finish. Our applause, camaraderie, and laughter continued throughout the celebratory evening.

The occasion was more than an opportunity to savor a remarkable achievement. It marked the end of a time when seventy-three wildly disparate young men stepped outside themselves and their own personal interests to coalesce into a team—a team unified by the goal of proving so many people so wrong.

Atlantic Coast Conference official Marvin Francis presented the championship trophy to captains Win Headley and Gary Winrow. Beaming with pride, they held it aloft to a chorus of cheers, whistles, and applause.

When the audience finally quieted down, Cal Stoll, the consummate optimist and the mastermind behind our championship season, stepped up to the microphone. The room fell silent.

"I have been asked how and when this started," he began. "I say it happened a year ago last spring with a group of young people. The squad grew smaller in size but bigger in heart as the tough spring practice went on.

"I told the players at our first spring practices in 1969 what champions do and what losers do not like to do. There was no way to make sprints and down-ups enjoyable, but that was not the point. The point was that there were enough players with enough heart, willingness to work hard, and discipline to believe they could get the job done."

He took a breath, paused, and then directed his gaze at us. "I hope what you have learned will carry on long after your trophies and awards are forgotten, those mugs have been lost, those watches have stopped working, and your collections of clippings are yellowed and packed away. I hope that the special feeling of love you had for each other this year will remain in your hearts. That was what being a member of this team meant."

Then he urged each of us to "take what you've learned and do something with it off the football field."

After that magical season, we moved on with our lives. The ACC championship was not our only feat, nor did it define who we became in the real world. But to every single one of us who made it through those two years, it brought a deep sense of personal accomplishment—an indescribable feeling of pride we would cherish forever. And when we are together, we don't have to say a thing.

EPILOGUE

The Man Behind the Miracle

By Charlie Dayton, *Old Gold and Black*

ootball, 1970 style, is now past history for all but a few fortunate bowl teams. For some, like South Carolina, the fall brought nothing but bitter disappointment after high preseason build-ups. For others, the season brought what had more or less been expected. In the case of #1 Texas, this was a 10-0 record or, for Holy Cross, an 0-10 mark. And for a small sprinkling of schools, football, 1970 style, exceeded the wildest expectations. In the latter group belong the Wake Forest Demon Deacons.

By this time, anything said about the Deacon Miracle of 1970 may seem superfluous. Most everyone is familiar with the stories of Larry Russell, Larry Hopkins, or Win Headley. Still, there is one more chapter In the Wake success story that should be told before the fairy tale book of 1970 Deacon football is closed. This is the story behind all of the success—the story of Coach Cal Stoll.

Much of the story about Stoll is no secret. Throughout the nation, he has been applauded for what many feel is the finest collegiate coaching job this fall. For his efforts, Coach Stoll has been awarded numerous honors, including

ACC Coach of the Year and District Coach of the Year. If National Coach of the Year is picked on the basis of the job done with talent available, Stoll would also have to be awarded this honor. But it will probably once again go to a coach like Darrell Royal at Texas, where success is inevitable.

But the awards, while honoring Stoll, fail to capture the man. While revealing that Stoll has been successful, awards and titles do not disclose the motivation behind that success. To discover this, one must talk to Cal Stoll. One must see the intensity of his personality. One must feel his aversion towards failure. Only after talking to Coach Stoll, can one realize how he could take a team supposedly destined for last and guide it to a championship.

In many ways, the 1970 Wake Forest football team was similar to Cal Stoll. In the beginning, neither was given much of a chance for success, only to prove later that hard work and determination can overcome many apparent shortcomings.

Stoll's inaugural year included a 3-7 record and lopsided defeats by such scores as 49-7. This fall was supposed to be no different, except that many said that it would be worse. When the football writers came to Wake Forest on their annual tour in August, Stoll brought laughter from the scribes by saying that Wake's goal in 1970 was winning the conference championship.

Obviously, the "experts" were not familiar with Coach Stoll nor the heart of the 1970 ACC Champions.

ABOUT THE
AUTHOR

Born June 9, 1949, in New Haven, Connecticut to Helen and Dante Doda, I was the youngest and only boy of five children. My childhood unfolded in nearby Derby, where I spent countless hours climbing trees and exploring the woods that bordered our neighborhood. These formative years instilled in me a sense of adventure, freedom, and fearlessness that would serve me well throughout life.

In 1960, our family relocated to Franklin Lakes, New Jersey, which became my teenage hometown and the springboard for my football career. At Ramapo Regional High School, I earned my place on the varsity team as a sophomore defensive end, marking the beginning of an athletic journey that would shape my future in unexpected ways.

My high school football career flourished over the next two years as I lettered in my junior and senior seasons, starting at offensive tackle and defensive end. The culmination of these efforts came when I was named captain of the 1966 team, an honor that coincided with recognition as an All-League, All-County, All-Area, and All-Suburban player.

My performance on the field caught the attention of college recruiters and, in 1967, I joined the Wake Forest University freshman class under the recruitment of Beattie Feathers during Bill Tate's coaching regime. The defining moment of my collegiate career came in 1970 when I earned a starting role at tight end before the Florida State game, as the Deacons transitioned to a two-tight-end, triple-option offense under Coach Cal Stoll.

I graduated from Wake Forest with a Bachelor of Science in Physics, reflecting my passion for understanding the fundamental laws of nature. This academic milestone was complemented by another significant event, my marriage to Nancy McIntyre, a wonderful woman who has been my steadfast partner through life's journey. Together, we've built a family that now includes two children and two grandchildren.

My pursuit of knowledge continued at the University of Florida, Gainesville, where I earned a Ph.D. in Physics in 1980. For the next fifteen years, I applied my scientific expertise in the defense contractor industry, contributing to projects that merged theoretical physics with practical applications.

In 1995, my career took an entrepreneurial turn when I founded an IT company, followed by a Software as a Service (SaaS) venture in 2011. Today I manage both companies remotely from the tranquil setting of Vermont, having relocated after thirty-two years in northern Virginia.

In July 2023, I made the decision to document our story, a narrative that encompasses not just my personal journey, but the experience of the entire 1970 Wake Forest Championship Team. This project represents my commitment to preserving the legacy of a group of ordinary athletes who achieved something extraordinary.

For those interested in learning more about the 1970 WFU Championship Team, I invite you to visit **www.wf70.com**, where you'll find:

- The complete 1970 Team Roster, including freshman and cheerleaders
- ACC Member Schools, 1970 statistics, and final standings
- The Team Picture, comments, and photographs from the 1970 season
- Tributes to teammates with us in spirit

Through this website and the story I've undertaken to tell, I hope to honor the memory of that exceptional season and the people who made it possible.

ACKNOWLEDGMENTS

I would like to express my deepest gratitude and appreciation for the support received throughout the writing of this book. This journey, much like our championship season itself, has been made possible only through the efforts of many individuals and institutions whose contributions deserve recognition.

No championship season exists in isolation. It lives on through the words and images captured by those who bore witness to our journey. *The Old Gold & Black* provided more than mere reporting, they created the historical record that has allowed me to revisit those moments with clarity and precision. Their detailed accounting of games, coupled with profound insights into the thoughts and emotions of players and coaches, preserved the authentic spirit of that once-in-a-lifetime season. Without their dedication to capturing both the statistical and human elements of our story, this book would lack the emotional texture that defined that transformative time.

The journalistic team whose words have informed these pages include:

- John Cooper, whose player profiles revealed the human stories behind the uniforms
- Charlie Dayton, whose editorial leadership kept our season in proper perspective
- Sue English, whose feature stories captured the spirit of campus during our run
- Tom Jennings, whose analytical mind translated complex game strategies for readers
- Gray Lawrence, whose contextual insights positioned our achievements within the broader college football landscape

- Larry Lyon, whose game recaps preserved the emotional highs and lows of each contest
- George Wright, whose editorial vision ensured comprehensive coverage of our season

Additional voices that added depth to the historical record include Bob Richards, whose photography captured decisive moments that words alone couldn't convey, and Neil S. Simstein, a '64 alumnus whose frame of reference bridged generations of Wake Forest football.

In the high-pressure world of sports journalism, Mary Garber of the *Winston-Salem Journal* and *Sentinel* stood apart. Her approach transcended conventional reporting, equal parts historian, storyteller, and compassionate observer. Mary possessed a rare gift: the ability to see beyond statistics and strategies to the human elements that made our team special. I can still picture Mary on the sidelines, notebook in hand, her eyes tracking not just the ball but the unfolding human drama. Where others saw only wins and losses, Mary discovered the subtle narratives that reveal character and connection. "Football is more than X's and O's," she once told me after a particularly punishing practice. "It's about the hearts beating inside those uniforms." Through her compelling narratives and insightful analysis, Mary elevated sports writing to an art form. By bringing to life our personal stories, sacrifices, breakthroughs, and moments of doubt and triumph, she created a lasting record that captures not just what we did, but who we were. I was truly blessed to know her. Her diligent work in chronicling our season transformed the writing of this book from uphill climb to genuine joy. Her legacy extends well beyond the pages of newspapers; it lives on in the rich, textured understanding of our championship season that she helped preserve. For those wishing to learn more about Mary's life and the countless barriers she broke in sports journalism, I encourage a visit to her tribute on our team's website: http://www.wf70.com/Tributes/Garber/Garber.tpl

Even the most carefully crafted manuscript benefits from the discerning eye of a gifted editor—and how profoundly true this proved to be. Acting on the wise counsel of a dear friend, I had the extraordinary fortune of asking Diana Weggler to serve as my editor, a decision that transformed this book. Diana proved to be nothing short of exceptional—a masterful editor whose razor-sharp intuition, editorial expertise, and meticulous attention to detail illuminated countless nuances that had escaped my notice despite having pored over every page countless times. Her ability to see what I could not, refine what I thought was already polished, and elevate every element of the manuscript was nothing less than remarkable. Working alongside Diana to transform this manuscript from a promising gem into a radiant jewel became one of the most rewarding and delightful experiences of this entire journey. Diana Weggler is that rare combination of consummate professional and treasured friend, and I am profoundly grateful to her. Contact Diana at **https://www.linkedin.com/in/dianalorenzweggler/**.

A book's cover serves as its first ambassador to the world. For creating a visual identity that captures both the effort and the thrill of our championship season, I am deeply grateful to Brittany Becker of BrittLouise Creative. Brittany's talent, adaptability, and creative vision transformed abstract concepts into a compelling visual representation of our story. During our initial consultation, her questions revealed a desire to understand not just the facts of our season, but also, its emotional landscape. The resulting cover design perfectly balances athletic dynamism with historical significance. The outstanding book cover she delivered does more than decorate our story, it invites readers into the world of Wake Forest football circa 1970. In addition, Brittany's professional design and layout of the interior makes for a read that is crisp, balanced, and visually pleasing. For those interested in experiencing Brittany's design sensibility firsthand, please visit: **http://www.brittlouisecreative.com**. Cover Photos: Football player © Pixabay/Pexels.com; Background stadium © **master1305/iStock.com**.

No acknowledgment would be complete without recognizing the central figures in this story, my teammates from the 1970 season. What we experienced together created a brotherhood that has withstood the test of time. As Coach Cal Stoll often reminded us, "Champions aren't made on game day. They're made in the thousands of moments when no one is watching." My teammates embodied this Stollism through their commitment to excellence in practice, in the weight room, in the classroom, and in life. I extend my deepest gratitude to all who wore the Gold and Black uniform alongside me. Your friendship has enriched my life beyond measure. Special thanks go to those who contributed their memories to this book, helping create a multidimensional portrait of our championship season.

Finally, I offer my heartfelt sympathy to the families and friends of those teammates no longer with us. Though they have departed physically, their spirits continue to provide inspiration for these pages. The lessons we learned together, about perseverance, unity, and the pursuit of excellence, constitute a legacy that transcends mortality. In many ways, this book serves as both celebration and memorial, a testament to what we achieved together and a tribute to the enduring impact of that magical season on all our lives.

www.ingramcontent.com/pod-product-compliance
Lightning Source LLC
Chambersburg PA
CBHW051420090426
42737CB00014B/2757